NYSTCE Health Education (073) Test

"You never fail until you stop trying" - Albert Einstein

For inquiries;
info@xmprep.com

NYSTCE Health Education (073) Test #1

Test Taking Tips

- ☐ Take a deep breath and relax
- ☐ Read directions carefully
- ☐ Read the questions thoroughly
- ☐ Make sure you understand what is being asked
- ☐ Go over all of the choices before you answer
- ☐ Paraphrase the question
- ☐ Eliminate the options you know are wrong
- ☐ Check your work
- ☐ Think positively and do your best

Table of Contents

TEST DIRECTION

DIRECTIONS

Read the questions carefully and then choose the ONE best answer to each question.

Be sure to allocate your time carefully so you are able to complete the entire test within the testing session. You may go back and review your answers at any time.

You may use any available space in your test booklet for scratch work.

Questions in this booklet are not actual test questions but they are the samples for commonly asked questions.

This test aims to cover all topics which may appear on the actual test. However some topics may not be covered.

Studying this booklet will be preparing you for the actual test. It will not guarantee improving your test score but it will help you pass your exam on the first attempt.

Some useful tips for answering multiple choice questions;

- Start with the questions that you can easily answer.

- Underline the keywords in the question.

- Be sure to read all the choices given.

- Watch for keywords such as NOT, always, only, all, never, completely.

- Do not forget to answer every question.

1

Alexa is bothered by her daughter's mental health since she has been showing signs of withdrawal and depression. She schedules a doctor appointment.

In this situation, which of the following additional actions is most significant for Alexa to take?

A) Study and search for therapy alternatives associated with teenage depression on the Internet to prepare for various diagnoses.
B) Strive to involve her daughter in a talking therapy wherein the mother assumes the position of a mental health counselor.
C) Spend a long weekend trip to provide a change of pace and scenery for her daughter.
D) Show her support. have constant communication with her, and observe for any bothersome behavior.

2

In order to have the occupational risks of workers monitored, the U.S government commonly use which of the following public health strategy?

A) Health facilities and laboratories are required to report occupational lung diseases, poisoning due to pesticide and metal, and radiation illness.
B) Training programs on hazardous substances like asbestos worker training and certification programs are conducted.
C) Anecdotal information and case studies that are reported by individual workers to the public health departments are collected.
D) The indoor and outdoor air quality and drinking water supplies are tested regularly in major urban areas of the United States.

3

Which of the following U.S. government agencies regulate the use of food additives?

A) Food and Drug Administration
B) Department of Health and Human Services
C) United States Department of Agriculture
D) United States Department of Trade and Industry

4

Pneumonia is a disease caused by bacteria and viruses in one or both lungs. This infection causes difficulty in breathing due to which of the following?

A) Swelling of the bronchial passages
B) Filling of the lungs with fluid
C) Tissue breakdown in the lungs
D) Loss of elasticity of the alveoli

5

What is the primary goal of food biotechnology?

A) To improve the health and safety of foods
B) To increase the productions of milk, meat, and other agricultural products
C) To clone agricultural products such as tomatoes
D) To develop foods for space explorations

6

The word "vitamin" was derived from the word "vitamine" that was coined in 1911 by the biochemist Casimir Funk (1884-1967). Vitamins are essential for regular growth and development of an organism. Vitamins must be consumed periodically and in a limited amount to avoid deficiency.

Which of the following about the vitamins is not correct?

A) Your body can also make vitamins D and K but if you eat a vegetarian diet you may need to take a vitamin B12 supplement because it is found in foods such as meat, fish, and dairy products.

B) Vitamin K is found naturally in vegetables, beans, eggs, strawberries and meat, and deficiency of Vitamin K can cause the risk of uncontrolled bleeding.

C) Water soluble vitamins (vitamin B and C) have to be taken in the diet more frequently than fat soluble vitamins.

D) Vitamin D (sometimes called the as the sunshine vitamin) is produced by the action of ultraviolet rays on the skin and the deficiency of Vitamin D is not widespread in US.

7

Most people worldwide are immediately affected by which of the following environmental issues?

A) Water pollution

B) Noise pollution

C) Air pollution

D) Land pollution

CONTINUE ▶

8

What is the most probably effect when overtraining in a college cross-country runner?

A) Increased lactate concentrations
B) Decreased creatine kinase
C) Increased muscle glycogen
D) Decreased percentage of body fat

9

Type II Herpes, or genital herpes, is an infection caused by the herpes simplex virus II (HSV-II) and is generally transmitted through sexual contact.

This disease is characterized by which of the following?

A) White pus-like secretion and discomfort during sexual intercourse
B) Pink to red cauliflower-shaped masses in or around the sex organ
C) Burning sensation when peeing
D) Clumps of tiny blisters around the genitals

10

All organized private and public measures aiming to prevent disease, promote health and prolong life among the population as a whole refers to Public Health.

Which of the following is not one of the core functions of public health?

A) Assessment, Policy development, and Assurance are three main functions of public health.
B) Assurance refers informing, educating and empowering the community.
C) Assessment refers monitoring health, diagnosing and investigating health problems.
D) Policy development refers improving the use of scientific knowledge to improve the communities health.

11

A woman has been exercising and running three miles several times a week for eight weeks. She noticed that the muscles on her legs had gained more endurance; however, there has been a slight difference in the muscles' strength.

The runner's observation best demonstrates which of the following principles of exercise and sports training?

A) The principle of specificity
B) The principle of adaptation
C) The principle of progression
D) The principle of reversibility

12

Diet, physical fitness, and individual health are interrelated with each other.

To better enhance a student's understanding of it, which of the following nutritional tools would most likely be useful?

A) The nutritional values of foods as well as the calories lost by different physical activities listed on appendixes and tables.
B) Understanding the relationship between nutrition and disease risk factors by reading medical journal articles.
C) Software programs capable of considering personal profiles to analyze food intake and activity levels.
D) The nutritional fact sheets for each major food group.

CONTINUE ▶

13

A teacher wants to improve his student's motivation and feelings of academic success.

Which of the following approaches would be the most effective in achieving this goal and helping students develop self-esteem?

A) Making a list of learning objectives for all students based on their weak areas
B) Helping students in developing their goals based on their strengths and needs
C) Giving the students an opportunity to share the benefits of their learning objectives with their friends
D) Reporting student's achievement to the parents and guardians

14

Isometric exercise is considered as a strength training in which the muscle length and joint angle do not change during contraction.

Which of the following is not correct about isometric exercise?

A) It can increase muscle strength at specific joint angles.
B) It contributes to building muscle and burning fat.
C) It always produces spikes in systolic blood pressure.
D) It can cause a life-threatening cardiovascular accident because it is done in one position without movement.

15

Alateen is a fellowship program for teenagers, whose lives have been affected by someone else's drinking.

Which of the following is the primary goal of the organization called Alateen?

A) Providing social support to teenagers affected by alcoholism in their families.

B) Developing alcohol recovery programs for teenagers.

C) Funding public high schools for their alcohol prevention programs.

D) Establishing partnerships with public agencies in communities to cope with alcoholism.

16

Secondary prevention's goal is to reduce the progression of disease or any health related issue that an individual already has and does not know it.

Which of the following information about secondary prevention is not correct?

A) Secondary prevention is done by treating disease or injury as soon as possible to stop or slow its progress.

B) Implementing chronic disease management and rehabilitation programs are examples of secondary prevention.

C) Daily diet and exercise programs to prevent further heart attacks or strokes are examples of secondary prevention.

D) Regular screening tests to identify disease in its earliest stages like breast cancer screening are examples of secondary prevention.

CONTINUE ▶

17

Which of the following websites would help a community member most in searching the advantages and disadvantages of major health plans, prescription plans, and prevention and wellness programs?

A) AHRQ; Agency for Healthcare Research and Quality

B) WHO; World Health Organization

C) CDC; Centers for Disease Control and Prevention

D) OSHA; Occupational Safety and Health Administration

18

Anxiety refers to persistent and excessive feelings of tension, nervousness, anxious thoughts about many different things.

Anxiety is a very normal response to stressful life events, but when it becomes more substantial, then it interferes with your life and can cause serious mental health problems.

Which of the following about anxiety is not correct?

A) Anxiety causes the body to feel fatigue, restlessness, or sweating.

B) Lack of concentration, racing thoughts, or unwanted thoughts is the cognitive symptoms of anxiety.

C) Anxiety disorders are among the most common mental disorders in the United States.

D) It's possible to develop generalized anxiety disorder as an adult, but children do not exhibit anxiety.

19

Maggie's blood test result shows that she has a high cholesterol level. Her doctor Nicole gives Maggie some advice about the ways to lower her cholesterol.

Considering that Maggie has a partner, by which of the following ways can her partner influence her effectively for a healthy lifestyle?

A) Give Maggie a gym membership and encourage her to work out regularly.

B) Give Maggie self-help nutritional books from the library.

C) To obtain high accuracy for the next test on the follow-up check-up, Maggie's partner needs to ensure that she fasts before having the test.

D) Show support to Maggie's new healthy lifestyle instructed by her doctor by also doing what Maggie is doing such as eating low-fat, high-fiber meals each day.

20

The human body utilizes fat as an energy source since it is the primary storage of energy in the body. The body requires a sufficient amount of fat for good health; however, consuming too much fat may be unhealthy.

Among the methods listed, which of the following can most accurately determine a person's body fat content?

A) Calculating the circumference of hips, waist, thighs, and arms

B) Underwater weighing or hydrostatic weighing

C) Scales and a height-weight chart

D) Skin-fold calipers

CONTINUE ▶

21

Which of the following would a 15-year-old girl most likely feel if she had trouble making friends in her new school?

A) Glad she left her old school
B) Excited
C) Proud
D) Socially inadequate

22

The government conducts various prevention programs regarding substance abuse.

Among these programs aimed at preventing substance abuse, which of the following is the least effective?

A) Life-skills training
B) Value clarification
C) Teaching awareness about the effects of substance abuse.
D) Teaching how to develop self-esteem

23

Food and Drug Administration, or FDA, is a federal agency that is responsible for protecting and improving public health. It requires U.S. food corporations to include additives in specific food products, such as folate in grain products and iodine in salt.

Which of the following is a primary objective of these types of policies?

A) To counterbalance the food proteins that induce allergic reactions to some people and produce antibodies.
B) To assure that Americans get the needed daily intake of all vital micronutrients.
C) To decrease the need for adding food preservatives food to limit spoilage.
D) To reduce the health risks associated with nutrient deficiencies such as cardiovascular problems and congenital disabilities.

CONTINUE ▶

24

Which of the following defines HAACP?

A) An agency in the government that controls the price of goods in the market
B) A list of guidelines for training employees in the food industry
C) A list of guidelines for ensuring food safety in processing, packaging, distribution, storage, and preparation
D) The agency in the government that inspects truth labeling in commercial products

25

Immunization is a very important primary prevention.It is the ability of an organism to resist a specific infection by the specific antibodies or white blood cells.

Which of the following about immunity is not correct?

A) Human immune system produces antibodies specifically to fight a particular invading substance.
B) Breast feeding is very important for an infant because antibodies in breast milk allow the passive transfer of immunity from mother to baby.
C) AIDS (acquired immunodeficiency syndrome) is caused by the human immunodeficiency virus (HIV) in which the immune system is too weak to fight off infection.
D) Immunity acquired after an infection is called as innate immunity and passive immunity is obtained through injection of antibodies.

CONTINUE ▶

26

Which of the following explains why the Physicians' Desk Reference (PDR) Consumer Drug Information online database is regularly consulted?

A) To investigate marketing methods and to promote newly registered drugs.
B) To collect data on the prices imposed by local drugs stores.
C) To collect information on proper dosages, side effects, and potential interactions of specific drugs.
D) To find the lists of drugs approved and covered by particular health insurance policies.

27

Flexibility can also be called as limberness. It is the range of movement in a joint or series of joint, and length in muscles that cross the joints inducing a bending motion.

Which of the following factors does not affect flexibility?

A) Age
B) Gender
C) Practice Level
D) Connective muscles

28

Stretching is an exercise in which certain muscle or group of muscles is stretched or flexed so that the muscle's felt elasticity is improved and comfortable muscle tone is achieved.

Which of the following is not a type of stretching?

A) Isometric stretch
B) Muscular stretch
C) Relaxed stretch
D) Active stretch

29

Defibrillation is a method used in medicine to stop ventricular fibrillation or pulseless ventricular tachycardia. It utilizes an electric shock to allow the restoration of the heart's normal rhythm.

Which of the following factors should be ensured first before doing automated external defibrillation on a heart attack victim?

A) No one must be in direct contact with the victim.
B) There must be sufficient inclination to the victim's head.
C) The victim's arms should be in a secured position.
D) There must be an ambulance nearby.

CONTINUE ▶

30

Body organs perform specific actions in the human body.

The discharge of liquid wastes in the body is the primary function of which organ?

A) Kidneys

B) Small Intestine

C) Skin

D) Lungs

31

Many programs or activities are made to reduce alcoholism as well as the drug abuse within a community.

Which of the following actions would have the least effect on controlling alcoholism and drug abuse?

A) Increasing the number of law enforcers near the schools.

B) Limiting the number of bars within a community by having zoning ordinances.

C) Implementing drug prevention programs with the parents and students as the target audience.

D) Putting high taxes on tobacco products and alcoholic beverages.

32

Incomplete proteins lack in one or more amino acids that are important in building cells.

Which of the following is not a dietary source of an incomplete protein?

A) Eggs

B) Legumes

C) Nuts

D) Grains

33

The constant exposure of humans or other organisms to high sound levels which may result in adverse effects is referred to as **noise pollution**.

Which of the following health problems will most likely result from noise pollution?

A) Illnesses that are stress-related

B) Chemical hypersensitivities

C) Dizziness and visual disorders

D) Obsessive compulsive disorders (OCD)

34

Some psychosocial disorders may develop or first become apparent during adolescence.

Which of the following psychosocial problems are more common among girls during adolescence?

A) Mood disorders
B) Lack of self control
C) Antisocial behavior
D) Eating disorders

35

People are obsessed with losing weight. Health experts reveal that a person must burn 3,500 calories to lose one pound.

Physical Activity	Calories Burned per Hour
Aerobics	500
Bicycling	590
Dancing	330
Walking	460

Which of the following activities can make an individual lose one pound (Refer to the information given above)?

A) Half an hour of bicycling every day for one week
B) An hour of dancing every day for one week
C) Half an hour of walking every day for one week
D) An hour of aerobics every day for one week

36

Which of the following describes the behaviors of an adolescent who displays a consistent depressive mood and significant susceptibility to stress?

A) Normal feelings which are expected for adolescents.
B) Hormonal changes associated with puberty results in these behaviors.
C) Personal risk factors which are associated with substance abuse.
D) Risk factors which are associated with participation in a deviant subculture.

CONTINUE ▶

37

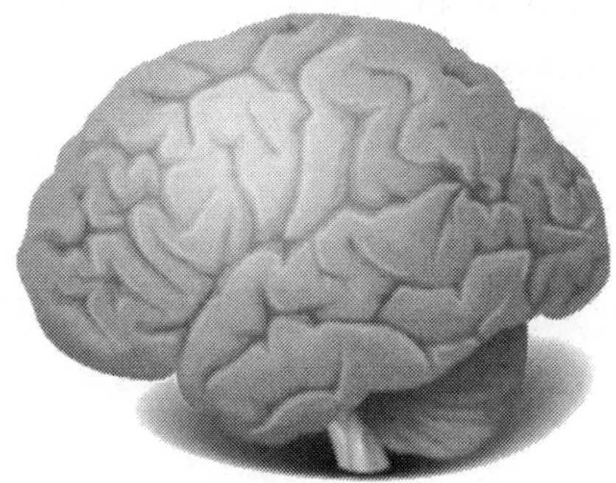

The **brain** is an organ that acts as the central nervous system. Some of its primary function are the processing of information and releasing hormones. A specific part of the brain is responsible for determining the reaction of the body to stress and acts as the sympathetic nervous system's control center.

Which of the following parts of the brain is responsible for the functions mentioned above?

A) Prefrontal cortex
B) Corpus callosum
C) Cerebellum
D) Hypothalamus

38

Which of the following mental disorder is most frequently diagnosed in the United States?

A) Mood disorder which is a psychological disorder characterized by the elevation or lowering of a person's mood.
B) Anxiety disorder which means having regular or uncontrollable worries about many different things in your everyday life.
C) Eating disorder which is characterized by abnormal or disturbed eating habits.
D) Substance abuse which means being dependent on an addictive substance, especially alcohol or drugs.

39

Which of the following diseases is considered one of the most common sexually transmitted infections in the United States and is very serious since it usually shows no symptoms until subsequent damage occurs?

A) Syphilis: A sexually transmitted disease (STD) bacterial infection caused by bacteria
B) Herpes simplex: An infection that is caused by a herpes simplex virus (HSV)
C) Chlamydia: A sexually transmitted disease (STD) which is easily spread because it often causes no symptoms
D) Gonorrhea: A sexually transmitted disease (STD) that can affect the female reproductive tract and vagina.

40

Which of the following statements best describes the American Red Cross?

A) It is an organization that aims to assist in emergency and disaster relief.
B) It is a non-profit health foundation that aims to the enhance health.
C) It is a health association that aims to improve the national health information services.
D) It is an organization that aims to protect the consumers in the health-care marketplace.

41

Vitamin K molecules consists of structurally similar, fat-soluble vitamins such as phylloquinone (Vitamin K1), menaquinone (Vitamin K2), and menadione (Vitamin K3). It is found mainly in green leaves.

Which of the following is the importance of Vitamin K in the human body?

A) It is crucial for the absorption of minerals.
B) It is needed for maintaining the good condition of the skin tissues.
C) It is needed for bone formation.
D) It is vital for blood clotting.

CONTINUE ▶

42

Cardiovascular disease refers to diseases involving the heart or blood vessel particularly, a narrowed or blocked blood vessel which may result in complications such as heart attack. Adolescents, in particular, are advised to take active steps to avoid having cardiovascular disease.

Which of the following best describes the reason to this?

A) The risk of developing cardiovascular disease is greatly influenced by things done during adolescence.

B) Using standard diagnostic tools for detecting cardiovascular disease is not effective in adolescents.

C) The risk factors for adolescents are prevalent as compared with other age groups.

D) Treating cardiovascular disease in adolescents and young adults are hard to manage and control.

43

Headache is pain that may occur on one or both sides of the head and it affects the quality of life.

Which of the following is associated with stress-related headaches?

A) Eating foods such as nuts and chocolates cause a reaction due to proteins present on them.

B) The blood vessels that lead to the brain is constricting.

C) The muscles on the neck as well as the back of the head are experiencing sustained contractions.

D) The level of glucose in the bloodstream is decreased.

CONTINUE ▶

44

Drugs are substances that exhibit a physiological effect when ingested or introduced to the body.

Which of the following drug types can most possibly create physical dependence when used?

A) Barbiturates: Drugs that act as a central nervous system depressant

B) Inhalants: Medicinal preparations that produce chemical vapors for inhaling.

C) Steroids: Drugs used to relieve swelling and inflammation, such as prednisone and cortisone

D) Hallucinogens: Drugs that alter perception (awareness of surrounding objects and conditions), thoughts, and feelings.

45

Which of the following information does Health History Questionnaire collect?

A) Evidence of disclosure

B) Previous exercise history

C) Detailed medical report form doctor

D) Fitness measurement data

46

Some common **pathogens** are viruses, bacteria, fungi, protozoa, and worms.

Which of the following about a pathogen is correct?

A) It is a kind of protein which produces antibodies.

B) It is necessary for body function.

C) It can be seen without a microscope.

D) It is anything that can cause disease.

47

Fiber absorbs water on its way through the digestive systems and results in a softer stool. Because of this property of fiber, eating fiber-rich foods reduces the risk of which of the following?

A) Hypertension

B) Hemorrhoids

C) Heart disease

D) Osteoporosis

CONTINUE ▶

48

Considering the recent case of an international traveler with a resistant TB, which of the following problem constituted by globalization can this case be an example of?

A) Lack of international centers for disease control.

B) Differences between global healthcare management.

C) Insufficient international health insurance plan.

D) The danger of spreading of dangerous pathogens as well as contagious disease.

49

Cancer is defined as the group of diseases that involves the abnormal growth of cells with the ability to migrate and spread to other parts of the body.

Which of the following options best illustrates the three general warning indications of cancer?

A) Abnormal bleeding, unhealed sores, and the appearance of lumps on the body

B) Extreme headaches, light sensitivity, and development of cataract

C) Weight loss, weakness and exhaustion, and swelling of the joints

D) Nausea and vomiting, severe muscle spasms, and pressure in the chest

50

Depression is a common and serious medical illness which is characterized as a mood disorder that causes a persistent feeling of sadness and loss of interest for long periods of time.

Which of the following is the most common symptom of depression?

A) High anxiety in daily life activities.

B) Extreme fears that are not realistic.

C) Eating too much and sleeping too much.

D) Loss of interest and pleasure in ordinary activities including sex.

51

Gina has an average daily intake of 175g of protein, 350g of carbohydrate, and 100g of fat. What percent of Gina's total calorie intake is protein?

A) 23.3%

B) 28%

C) 30.2%

D) 45%

CONTINUE ▶

52

Which of the following best describes the importance of the ozone layer in the upper atmosphere?

A) The ozone layer absorbs harmful ultraviolet radiation.

B) It leads to a reduction on the amount of acid rain as well as urban smog.

C) Enhancement of the greenhouse effect

D) It is responsible for the increase in all types of skin cancer.

53

One of the symptoms of having an eating disorder is having abnormal or disturbed eating habit like anorexia nervosa.

Which of the following is considered first if a student has an eating disorder?

A) Check the weight regularly

B) Make sure to have a balanced diet in place

C) Refer the student to the doctor

D) Monitor the food intake

54

When drinking water is contaminated with nitrate it is transformed to nitrite in the digestive system. The nitrite oxidizes the iron in the hemoglobin of the red blood cells and forms methemoglobin, which decreases the oxygen-carrying ability of hemoglobin.

Which of the following sources of pollution can be controlled to reduce the high levels of nitrites and nitrates in drinking water?

A) Septic systems of the buildings.

B) Agricultural runoff originating from the fields and feedlots

C) Wastewater discharged by heavy industry

D) Treated wastewater released by the municipal sewage-treatment plants

55

Overtraining means having a continuous intense training that does not allot enough recovery time.

Which of the following is not a byproduct of overtraining?

A) Imbalance between exercise and recovery

B) Training exceeds psychological and physiological capacity of a person

C) Can have negative effect on strength training

D) Always results in injury or illness

CONTINUE ▶

56

Which of the following statements best describes the reason why daily dental flossing is highly recommended?

A) Dental flossing prevents formation of plaque .
B) It helps removing the food particles trapped in between the teeth which may result in tooth decay.
C) It is crucial in maintaining the space between the teeth to avoid crowding of the teeth.
D) Dental flossing prevents bad breath.

57

Which of the following elements in the hemoglobin (a protein found in red blood cells) is responsible for binding oxygen?

A) Calcium
B) Iron
C) Magnesium
D) Titanium

58

There are different Government Agencies involved in Health Issues. Which of the following about the golas of these agencies is not correct?

A) Environmental Protection Agency (EPA) examines environmental health issues and makes recommendations.
B) Department of Agriculture & the FDA protects the nation's food supply.
C) Department of Homeland Security sets radiation safety standards for nuclear power plants and other sources of energy.
D) Occupational Safety and Health Administration (OSHA) aims to reduce injuries and hazardous exposures in the workplace

59

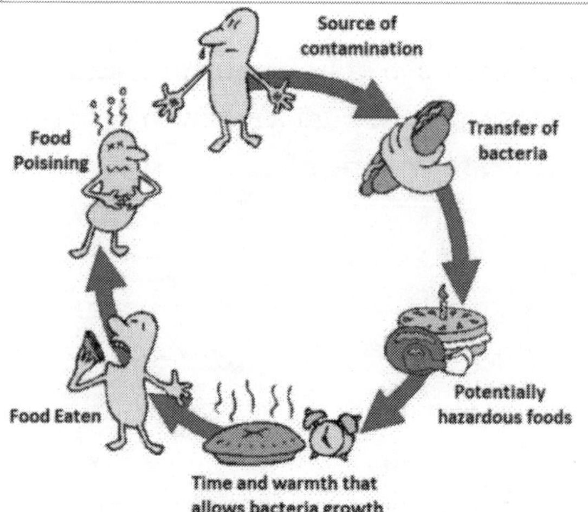

Food contamination is a common problem when mishandling food during food preparation and may cause health problems to consumers. To prevent food contamination, there are rules set to be followed strictly.

Which of the following is the most important food preparation and storage practice followed to prevent food contamination?

A) During food preparation, always use a porous wood cutting board.
B) The eggs, milk, and cheese or any dairy product should be placed in the coldest parts of the refrigerator.
C) Do not put raw meat and seafood alongside other foods when preparing.
D) Avoid eating leftover foods stored in the refrigerator for more than two days.

60

Minerals are substances that occur naturally on Earth.

Which of the following is an example of minerals?

A) Sunlight
B) Vitamin B12
C) Vitamin D
D) Iron

61

When attempting to control a wound from bleeding, which of the following methods should be used first?

A) Making a tourniquet and putting it on the wound.
B) Applying pressure to the cut and elevating the bleeding portion.
C) Placing pressure indirectly to the wound by putting the thumb on the pressure area.
D) Utilizing an air splint to form a pressure bandage.

62

Its mission is to ensure that employees work in a safe and healthful environment by setting and enforcing standards.

Which of the following U.S government agencies is responsible for the establishment and implementation of standards mentioned above?

A) Center for Disease and Control Prevention
B) National Labor Relation Board
C) Occupational Safety and Health Administration
D) National Institutes of Health

CONTINUE ▶

63

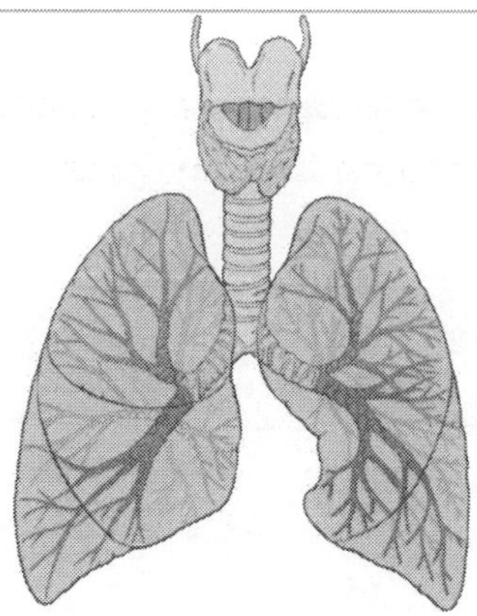

__________ pressure is required to be generated within the thoracic cavity in order for the diaphragm to contract. In this condition, the lungs would tend to ___________.

Which of the following terms correctly complete the statements given about how lungs work?

A) Negative, Expand
B) Positive, Expand
C) Positive, Contract
D) Negative, Contract

64

- Transport of pathogens across borders
- Population movement
- Technological variations related to the mass production of food
- The resistance of pathogens to antibiotics

The details given above best illustrates the factors affecting which of the following?

A) Diagnosis and control of long-term diseases
B) Incidence and prevalence of developing diseases
C) Transmission of degenerative diseases
D) Treatment of infectious illnesses

65

A **divorce** between two people can cause emotional stress, especially in children. During the time that the family structure is changing, which of the following approaches can effectively help the children handle this stressor?

A) Transferring to a new neighborhood to make a new start
B) Keeping a stable routine at home and in school
C) Spending more time with family and friends
D) Reading and consulting books about family life

66

If a person who engages in vigorous physical activity in which of the following there will be an increase?

A) Resting heart rate
B) Coronary thrombosis
C) Low density lipoproteins
D) High density lipoproteins

67

Which of the following is the main reason for the detorioration of cartilage and bone at skeletal joints?

A) Excessive work out
B) Excessive body weight
C) Lack of minerals such as calcium
D) Blood circulation problems

68

A child's growth and development, as well as energy needs, can be fulfilled by which of the following dietary patterns?

A) Eating carbohydrate-rich foods to counter any change in blood sugar levels.
B) Avoiding foods containing fats to prevent problems with vitamin and mineral absorption.
C) Eating small meals for the day which consists of carbohydrates, fats, proteins, vitamins, minerals, and water for the day.
D) Consuming a large, well-balanced meal throughout the day for the energy needs during the day's activities and comfortable sleep at night.

69

Check on the victim and do not move him unless necessary. If the person shows no signs of life, such as breathing, coughing or movement then you can begin CPR.

In which of the following positions a shock victim should be placed before giving first aid?

A) In a semi-sitting position
B) On his back with the legs elevated
C) On his back with the head elevated
D) In the recovery position, on his side

70

Hemophilia is a disorder wherein the blood cannot clot properly and may lead to continuous bleeding. **Sickle-cell disease**, on the other hand, is a blood disorder that affects hemoglobin.

These diseases can be used to show the relationship between which of the following?

A) Aging and the development of persistent diseases
B) Lifestyle practices and the growth of disease
C) Environmental factors and the progress of chronic disease
D) Hereditary factors and the evolution of disease

71

Public Health prevents epidemics and the spread of disease, protects against environmental hazards, prevents injuries, promotes and encourages healthy behaviors, responds to disasters and assists communities in recovery, assures the quality and accessibility of health services.

Which of the following about the diseases is not correct?

A) Tuberculosis (TB) is primarily an airborne disease which is spread person -to-person through the air.

B) Obesity, Type 2 diabetes and Cardiovascular diseases are related to over-nutrition

C) Chlamydia is a sexually transmitted diseases which has the lowest incidence in the United States.

D) Cholera is an infectious disease caused by a bacterium resulting in severe diarrhea and dehydration that can result in death; was thought to be caused by miasma.

72

Public Health means Prevent, Promote and Protect.The goal of public health is to prevent disease and disability.

Which of the following about public health is not correct?

A) Government, health care professionals, and community members are responsible for public health.

B) Preventing epidemics and injuries, protecting against environmental hazards, and promoting healthy behaviors are some of the purposes of public health.

C) A principle of public health is that the health of the individual is not tied to his/her community.

D) If necessary to protect the health of the public, a public health officer may confine an individual to detention or prison.

CONTINUE ▶

73

Mary used to take on too many tasks and activities. However recently, she is refusing to participate new activities.

Which of the following is Mary exhibiting?

A) Multitasking
B) Time management
C) Laziness
D) Procrastination

74

Epidemiology is the study of the distribution and determinants of health-related events, and the control of diseases and other health problems.

Which of the following about epidemiology is not correct?

A) Louis Pasteur is the father of medicine who introduced the term "epidemic"
B) Pandemic is the epidemic affecting a large number of people, many countries, continents, or regions worldwide.
C) Epidemiologists generally use the incidence rate to refer to the number of new cases of a disease in a population within a specified time period.
D) John Snow is the father of epidemiology who provided an example of both a descriptive and analytic epidemiological study.

75

Which of the following elements in the hemoglobin (a protein found in red blood cells) is responsible for binding oxygen?

A) Calcium
B) Iron
C) Magnesium
D) Titanium

76

Which of the following order of the female reproductive parts shows the sperm's pathway towards the site of fertilization?

A) Urethra, Vagina, Fallopian tube, Uterus
B) Vagina, Cervix, Fallopian tube, Uterus
C) Vagina, Uterus, Fallopian tube, Cervix
D) Vagina, Cervix, Uterus, Fallopian tube

CONTINUE ▶

77

There are three distinct types of muscles in the human body; skeletal, cardiac, and smooth. Each type of muscle tissue has a unique structure and a specific role. Skeletal muscle moves bones and other structures, the Cardiac muscle contracts the heart to pump blood, the smooth muscle tissue forms organs like the stomach and changes shape to facilitate body functions.

Which of the following muscles in the human body function voluntarily?

A) Smooth
B) Cardiac
C) Sarcomere
D) Skeletal

78

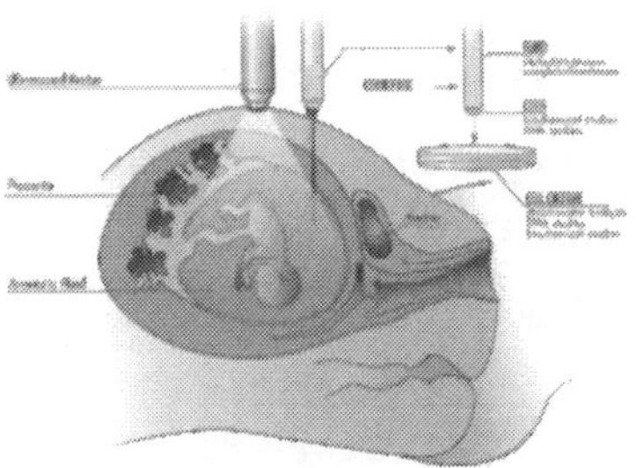

Amniocentesis is a medical procedure that involves getting a sample of the amniotic fluid, which contains cells from the fetus, and will be subjected for analysis. It is typically performed between 14 and 20 weeks.

Which of the following is amniocentesis often used?

A) For determining if there are certain disabilities present on a fetus
B) For estimating the potential of a woman to handle pregnancy to a term
C) For measuring the capability of transplant recipients in terms of immune response
D) For facilitating artificial insemination

79

A patient caught a bacterial infection. He has a high fever and has been experiencing chest pains, persistent cough, chills, and fluid accumulation.

The early stages of this disease would be most receptive in which of the following types of treatment?

A) Vaccinations
B) Vitamin supplements
C) Antibiotics
D) Cortisone shots

80

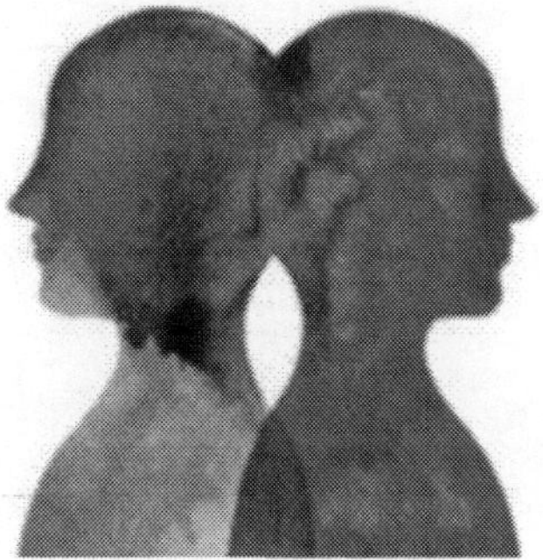

Mood disorders is a group of mental conditions that is mainly caused by disturbances in an individual's mood.

Which of the following gives the two common types of mood disorders?

A) Bipolar and tripolar disorders
B) Schizophrenia and depression
C) Biological and psychosocial disorders
D) Bipolar and unipolar disorders

81

Anabolism, constructive metabolism, is the synthesis of complex molecules in living organisms from simpler ones together with the storage of energy.

Which of the following is an example of anabolism?

A) The disintegration of proteins into amino acids
B) Disintegration of large molecules into smaller molecules
C) Forming of small molecules from large molecules
D) Forming of proteins from amino acids

82

Hormones have several functions in the human body. What is the hormone that is responsible for reducing inflammation and also known as "stress hormone"?

A) Insulin
B) Testosterone
C) Growth hormone
D) Cortisol

CONTINUE ▶

83

In response to a heavy loading session, which of the following exercises requires the longets recovery time for the stressed muscle groups?

A) Knee extension
B) Bench press
C) Front squat
D) Dumbbell fly

84

Which of the following is correct about anxiety?

A) Most antidepressant drugs can treat anxiety disorders.
B) The person can perform at his best when he is anxious and fearful.
C) Most people diagnosed with anxiety disorders have less activity in the fear circuit of their brains.
D) Most people diagnosed with anxiety disorders can live normal lives without treatment.

85

Absolute strength is the maximal force that a person can exert no matter how big or small is a person's muscle or body.

Which of the following statements about absolute strength is true?

A) Generally, women have about one third the strength of men.
B) Women can exert the same amount of strength as men.
C) Generally, women have about half the strength of men.
D) Generally, women have about two thirds the strength of men.

86

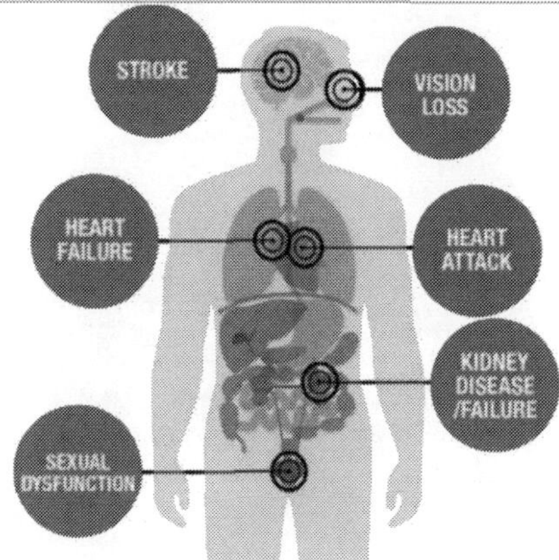

Who among the persons listed below is prone to heart disease?

A) Ben, a 32 year-old man with 130/70 mmHg
B) Sheena, an 18 year-old girl with 120/80 mmHg
C) James, a 38 year-old man with 121/81 mmHg
D) Jonas, a 37 year-old man with 140/90 mmHg

CONTINUE ▶

87

The physical activity of low to high intensity that is dependent on the aerobic energy-generating process is called aerobic exercise. Breathing and heart rate increases during an aerobic exercise session so that blood containing oxygen is distributed to the working muscle.

What factor is increased that causes the stimulation of pumping of blood?

A) Hemoglobin
B) Cardiac output
C) Blood glucose
D) Plasma volume

88

Which of the following refers to the state of physical, emotional, intellectual, and spiritual depletion characterized by feelings of helplessness and hopelessness?

A) Traumatization
B) Fatigue
C) Negativeness
D) Burnout

89

Which of the following is not the function of the cardiovascular system in the human body?

A) To oxygenate the blood through gas exchange.
B) To transport nutrients, gases and waste products around the body.
C) To protect the body from infection and blood loss.
D) To help the body maintain constant body temperature (thermoregulation)

90

By which of the following are the muscle fiber receptors at the neuromuscular junction stimulated?

A) Creatine phosphate
B) Calcium ions
C) Acetylcholine
D) Adenosine triphosphate (ATP)

CONTINUE ▶

91

In response to a heavy loading session, which of the following exercises requires the longets recovery time for the stressed muscle groups?

A) Knee extension
B) Bench press
C) Front squat
D) Dumbbell fly

92

The number associated with a specific type of food that indicates the food's effect on a person's blood sugar level is called the **glycemic index.**

After an exercise session of Paul, which of the following food should he consume for the highest glycemic index to replenish glycogen stores?

A) Green beans
B) Mashed potatoes
C) Orange juice
D) Yogurt

93

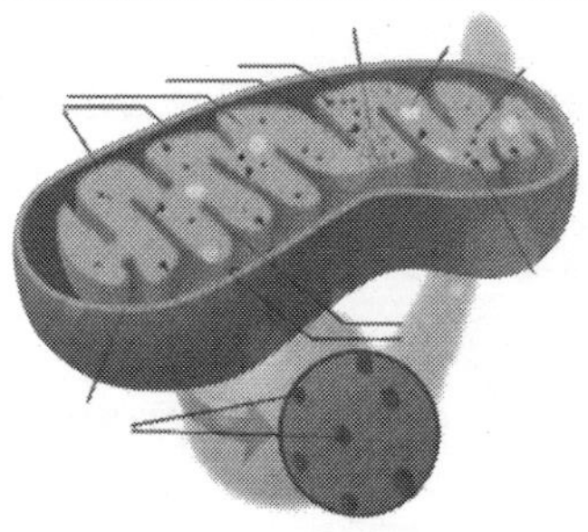

After aerobic training and resistance training, how does the density of mitochondria change?

A) After aerobic training it decreases and after resistance training it increases
B) After aerobic training it increases and after resistance training it decreases
C) For both trainings it increases
D) For both trainings it decreases

94

Plyometric exercises are considered as an effective way to improve strength and speed which is beneficial for sports training.

Which of the following is the most appropriate surface when performing high-intensity, low body plyometric drills?

A) Artificial turf
B) Grass field
C) Mini trampoline
D) Indoor basketball court

95

What do we call the sudden relaxation of muscle after experienceing high tension?

A) Muscle inhibition
B) Reciprocal inhibition
C) Mechanoreceptor
D) Autogenic inhibition

96

Fatigue is described as severe tiredness which is normally a result of physical or mental exertion.

Which of the following will result in the student to feel fatigue?

A) Depleted creatine phosphate
B) Sleep deprivation
C) Dehydration
D) Depleted muscle glycogen

97

Antibiotics are medicines used to treat a wide variety of infections or diseases caused by bacteria, such as respiratory tract infections, urinary tract infections, skin infections and infected wounds. Antibiotics have had both positive and negative impacts on society.

Which of the following can be considered as a negative impact of antibiotics?

A) New types of cancers have developed due to extensive use of antibiotics.
B) Over-abundance of medical professionals.
C) Increased obesity in humans due to use in consumer products.
D) Resistant strains of bacteria caused by extensive use of antibiotics.

CONTINUE ▶

98

Periodization is the systematic manipulation of the of the acute variables of training over a particular time that possibly ranges from days to years. Early eastern countries developed the original concept of periodization to improve the effectiveness of the adaptation of athletes to resistance training which usually revolves around the athlete's competitive calendar for him/her to be at his/her competitive peak for competition.

Which fo the following is the main idea behind periodization?

A) Changing the training type
B) Decrease resistance by 5%
C) Varying training intensity and volume
D) Exercising the appropriate muscles

99

One important human function is the mobility, and the loss of it, or immobility may lead to many physical problems and emotional problems. It can also lead to detrimental cardiac, muscular, respiratory, skeletal, urinary, gastrointestinal, skin and emotional changes.

Which of the following is an example of a skeletal hazard of immobility?

A) Contractures
B) Constipation
C) Calcium loss
D) Catabolism

100

What is the condition in which an excess of interstitial fluid would lead to swelling of the tissue?

A) Edema
B) Eczema
C) Hydration
D) Dehydration

CONTINUE ▶

SECTION 1 - GENERAL HEALTH

#	Answer	Topic	Subtopic	#	Answer	Topic	Subtopic	#	Answer	Topic	Subtopic	#	Answer	Topic	Subtopic
1	D	TC	SC2	26	C	TC	SC7	51	A	TC	SC4	76	D	TC	SC6
2	A	TC	SC3	27	D	TB	SB4	52	A	TC	SC5	77	D	TC	SC6
3	A	TC	SC4	28	B	TB	SB4	53	C	TC	SC4	78	A	TC	SC6
4	B	TC	SC7	29	A	TC	SC7	54	B	TC	SC5	79	C	TC	SC7
5	A	TC	SC4	30	A	TC	SC6	55	D	TB	SB4	80	D	TC	SC2
6	D	TC	SC4	31	A	TC	SC3	56	A	TC	SC1	81	C	TC	SC6
7	A	TC	SC5	32	A	TC	SC4	57	B	TC	SC6	82	D	TC	SC6
8	D	TB	SB4	33	A	TC	SC5	58	C	TC	SC3	83	C	TB	SB4
9	D	TC	SC7	34	D	TC	SC1	59	C	TC	SC4	84	A	TC	SC2
10	B	TC	SC3	35	D	TB	SB4	60	D	TC	SC4	85	D	TC	SC6
11	A	TB	SB4	36	C	TC	SC2	61	B	TC	SC7	86	D	TC	SC7
12	C	TC	SC4	37	D	TC	SC6	62	C	TC	SC5	87	B	TC	SC6
13	B	TC	SC2	38	B	TC	SC2	63	C	TC	SC6	88	D	TC	SC2
14	C	TB	SB4	39	C	TC	SC7	64	B	TC	SC7	89	A	TC	SC6
15	A	TC	SC3	40	A	TC	SC3	65	B	TC	SC2	90	C	TC	SC6
16	B	TC	SC3	41	D	TC	SC4	66	D	TB	SB4	91	C	TB	SB4
17	A	TC	SC3	42	A	TC	SC1	67	B	TB	SB4	92	B	TC	SC4
18	D	TC	SC2	43	C	TC	SC1	68	C	TC	SC4	93	B	TC	SC6
19	D	TC	SC4	44	A	TC	SC7	69	B	TC	SC7	94	B	TB	SB4
20	A	TB	SB4	45	C	TC	SC3	70	D	TC	SC7	95	D	TC	SC6
21	D	TC	SC2	46	D	TC	SC4	71	C	TC	SC3	96	D	TB	SB4
22	C	TC	SC4	47	B	TC	SC4	72	C	TC	SC3	97	D	TC	SC7
23	D	TC	SC7	48	D	TC	SC3	73	B	TC	SC1	98	C	TB	SB4
24	C	TC	SC4	49	A	TC	SC7	74	D	TC	SC3	99	C	TB	SB4
25	D	TC	SC3	50	D	TC	SC2	75	B	TC	SC4	100	A	TC	SC7

Topics & Subtopics

Code	Description	Code	Description
SB4	Health-Related Physical Fitness	SC5	Environmental Health
SC1	Personal Health	SC6	Anatomy & Physiology
SC2	Mental & Emotional Health	SC7	Health Promotion & Prevention of Injury and Diseases
SC3	Community Health	TB	Physical Education
SC4	Nutrition Health	TC	General Health

CONTINUE ▶

TEST DIRECTION

DIRECTIONS

Read the questions carefully and then choose the ONE best answer to each question.

Be sure to allocate your time carefully so you are able to complete the entire test within the testing session. You may go back and review your answers at any time.

You may use any available space in your test booklet for scratch work.

Questions in this booklet are not actual test questions but they are the samples for commonly asked questions.

This test aims to cover all topics which may appear on the actual test. However some topics may not be covered.

Studying this booklet will be preparing you for the actual test. It will not guarantee improving your test score but it will help you pass your exam on the first attempt.

Some useful tips for answering multiple choice questions;

- Start with the questions that you can easily answer.

- Underline the keywords in the question.

- Be sure to read all the choices given.

- Watch for keywords such as NOT, always, only, all, never, completely.

- Do not forget to answer every question.

CONTINUE ▶

1

If one day a parent becomes seriously ill, their children will be the most affected.

Which of the following will help children to cope with this type of situation effectively?

A) Give opportunities where feelings can be shown completely.

B) Attend psychotherapy every week to help in managing any changes in behavior.

C) Relieve stress by spending more time with extended family.

D) Research on medical treatments to understand them.

2

A person who is capable of understanding and applying acquired health information to personal health choices and behaviors has a better chance of managing a chronic disease.

Which of the following consequences has been the most closely related to inadequate health literacy among people diagnosed with Type 2 diabetes?

A) Engaging in diabetes learning programs

B) Struggling to maintain glycemic

C) Low percentage of diabetes-related dilemmas

D) Dealing with diabetes successfully

3

What should be the best range of maximum heart rate in terms of percentage in characterizing the student's exercise for health -related fitness in physical education class?

A) 85-100%

B) 60-85%

C) 40-60%

D) 20-40%

4

Information about public health is readily accessible for communal use. However, it can be occasionally confusing when deciding on what health products and services to utilize and which health behaviors to practice and execute.

Which of the following options is essential for people to make the most suitable judgments about their health?

A) Search and study health in internet websites.

B) Request for recommendations.

C) Acquire health insurance.

D) Be knowledgeable about health.

CONTINUE ▶

5

Intercultural communication refers to communication between people from different cultures or social groups verbally and nonverbally.

Which of the following would best describe the effect of intercultural communication?

A) Nonverbal expressions and behaviors may be interpreted in different ways by people of different cultures.
B) Cultural groups close to each other have fewest communication problems.
C) Communication desire must be higher on the majority culture comprising the group.
D) Communication and courtesy gestures are the same in all cultures.

6

The potential of a young man to become a perpetrator of violence is increased by which of the following risk factors?

A) Low connections with friends in the school
B) Being exposed to media that shows violence
C) Peer pressure that results in a negative feeling
D) Joining a social clique

7

Maria and Irah are childhood friends. Their homes are just a block away, and their parents happen to be high school friends too. However, all relationships undergo trials and misunderstanding. Maria poked up Irah's low grades in class causing them to become estranged. Maria feels sorry but doesn't know how to start a conversation since Irah always ignores her.

Which of the following could be the most useful communication method for them to help their relationship to have a fresh?

A) Telling both sides excuses on how the situation happened.
B) Assuming the situation didn't happen.
C) Undergoing counseling
D) Accepting responsibility about the situation

CONTINUE ▶

8

A **strain** is a stretching or tearing of muscle or tendon.

Which of the following will most likely to result in a muscle pull or strain?

A) Doing varying exercises every session
B) Interchanging work of upper and lower body every other day
C) Using static stretching rather than dynamic stretching to cool down after strength training
D) Exercising a particular muscle group without working for its opposing muscle group (e.g., quadriceps but not hamstrings)

9

Addiction is repeatedly engaging with drugs, alcohol, or gambling despite the harm it can cause since it has become a habit and source of pleasure. However, addicted users in a family can cause fear and hardship to the whole family.

Which of the following can be the most useful action in dealing with a family member's addiction to improve the family's wellness?

A) Confront the addicted family member about it since it will be a problem not only for him but through the family and seeking professional help for him.
B) Think of ways to adapt to the situation and let the addicted family member do his addiction until he regrets it.
C) Do everything not to have contact with the addicted family member since he can be harmful anytime.
D) Temporarily prioritize the addicted family needs over other family matters.

10

Kinesthesis is the ability of the person to feel movements of the limbs and body.

Which of the following is the other name for kinesthesis?

A) Proprioception
B) Coordination
C) Reflex action
D) Tonic neck response

11

Which of the following websites provides practical information to individuals, health professionals, nutrition educators, and the food industry to help consumers build healthier diets with resources and tools for dietary assessment, nutrition education, and other user-friendly nutrition information?

A) Nourished Kitchen
B) USDA ChooseMyPlate
C) Calorie Lab
D) Consumer Reports: Health

12

Nonverbal communication refers to communication that doesn't involve speaking. It can be through facial expressions, body language or facial expression.

Which of the following roles best illustrates nonverbal communication?

A) Reinforcing verbal communication
B) Reducing biases such as in cultures
C) Showing the needless of verbal communication
D) Avoiding misunderstanding through voice tone

13

Which of the following do you call a group of close relatives that live together or close to each other?

A) Foster family
B) Nuclear family
C) Blended family
D) Extended family

CONTINUE ▶

14

Adolescence refers to the transition period between childhood and adulthood that involves developmental changes in physical, intellectual, social and personality. It has been considered as a crucial stage in developing adaptable and logical thinking since this stage is where teens are faced with many issues and decisions.

Which of the following effects will most likely develop on an
adolescent's social development from a positive peer pressure through membership in a clique?

A) Creating a wide social network
B) Increasing communication skills
C) Comparing life challenges
D) Promoting feelings of competency

15

Greg and Megan are just started dating, and they are discussing their each other's responsibilities in the relationship.

Which of the following is an important responsibility of both of them?

A) Keeping their lines of communication open especially regarding issues and concerns about their relationship.
B) Always tabulating the good and bad sides of staying in a relationship.
C) Assessing one another based on how he or she is viewed by others.
D) Making a discussion about how they could support each other's long-term life plans.

CONTINUE ▶

16

Iris belongs to a family of five, with her siblings' ages ranging from 12 to 18. Five years ago, Iris' family lost their family home in a fire.

However, her family learned to cope with the changes caused by this crisis with the help of which of the following strategies?

A) Working with each other to deal with the situation at hand.

B) Designate one of the family members to be responsible for the decision-making.

C) Identifying the cause of the crisis that brought them the problem.

D) Depend on others for support.

17

Clique refers to a circle or group of people sharing common interests, views or features and spending time together.

Which of the following best describes why adolescents join clique?

A) Satisfy the need to have an alternative identity.

B) Gain high respect above others.

C) Expose themselves to a different environment.

D) Create larger connections.

18

Every weekend, Paul visits his parent's home together with his siblings for a weekly communication meeting where they discuss the issues or problems that they have and receive support from each other.

Which of the following does this kind of practice most likely influence in each family members?

A) The family member's ability to have their sense of fulfillment.

B) The family member's ability to prevent any negative behaviors.

C) The family member's ability to improve their problem-solving skills effectively.

D) The family member's ability to manage flexible patterns of behavior.

19

Mira is participating in a conflict resolution or peer mediation program.

Which of the following would Mira most likely learn first from attending the program in terms of managing anger?

A) How to express "I" statements effectively

B) How to listen carefully with respect

C) How to say "No" and be firm

D) How to think of different solutions and possibilities

20

The direct measurement of the rate of oxygen consumption during exercise is primarily determined by which of the following parameter?

A) VO2 max

B) Pulse rate

C) Minute ventilation

D) Red blood cell count

21

Which of the following do messages of a speaker that begin with "I" emphasize?

A) Making a person feel down for what he or she said.

B) Judging a person for something he or she made.

C) The emotions that resulted for the speaker are emphasized.

D) A person is assigned for commenting.

22

Wendy discovered that Christian, her ten-year-old son, stole candy from the grocery store.

To deal with this incident, which of the following behavior management practices should Wendy use?

A) Return to the store and pay for the item stolen to teach the child that stealing is not right.

B) Make the child write "Stealing is wrong" in a bond paper, back-to-back.

C) Do not give the child allowance as a payment for the stolen item.

D) Ban the child from doing his favorite activities for an indefinite period.

23

Addiction to drugs, alcohol, or gambling, affects not only the individual experiencing it but also the people surrounding him.

Which of the following can improve family wellness by dealing with a family member's addiction most effectively?

A) Try to avoid the family member that is suffering from addiction not to experience any difficulties caused by them.

B) Prioritize the addicted family member by focusing and giving all the attention he or she needs.

C) Any problems caused by addiction may be ignored by the family members.

D) Confront the addicted family member and ask for professional help.

24

Physical health is critical for overall well-being and is the most visible of the various dimensions of health, which also include social, intellectual, emotional, spiritual and environmental health.

Most personal traits are interdependent and changes in one may affect another. Which of the following personal traits is affected by your physical health?

A) Cultural background

B) Ethnic heritage

C) Self-confidence

D) Gender

25

What instrument can be used to determine an individual's body fat composition most effectively?

A) A skinfold caliper

B) Scales and a height-weight chart

C) Hydrostatic weighing

D) Measurements of the circumference of the waist, hips, thighs, and arms of the person.

CONTINUE ▶

26

In a situation wherein a child asks for her parents' advice on a certain matter about her school, which of the following best promotes a good and healthy relationship between the child and the parent?

A) Discussing the matter but making the final decision for the child.

B) Telling the child to ask for advice from the school guidance counselor instead.

C) Telling the child to ask for advice from the school teacher instead.

D) Showing support on the child's decision.

27

Severe illness is where a person has detrimental defects that affect his or her daily function, needs high case treatments due to complicated symptoms and has a high chance of mortality.

Which of the following approaches will be an essential initial step to help a child adjust to the situation wherein a parent falls seriously ill?

A) Provide opportunities to express feelings unconditionally.

B) Schedule with a psychotherapist as often as possible to handle emotional and behavioral changes.

C) Allow the child not to go to school and do leisure activities.

D) Allow extended family to be with the child to help them with his or her daily needs.

28

Which of the following domains of learning do learning about sports rules, traditions, history, and etiquette fall?

A) Interactions
B) Mental skills under cognitive
C) Physical skills under psychomotor
D) Emotional skills under affective

29

Kai and Jennie are newlyweds. They decided to build their house in the city considering the proximity of their location to their work address. Jennie is an only child, and her father died a few years ago leaving her mother alone in their ancestral house. Kai and Jennie asked her mother to live with them to lessen her sadness, and she accepts it too.

Which of the following types of diverse family structures is about to be created?

A) Adoptive
B) Polyamorous
C) Extended
D) Nontraditional

30

Upon opening her social media account, Risa, a high school student, receives a message from an anonymous sender containing lewd messages.

Which of the following did Risa experience?

A) Harassment: Unwelcome conduct that is based on race, color, religion, sex, and etc
B) Defamation: The action of damaging a third party's good reputation
C) Abuse: Treating someone with cruelty, especially regularly and repeatedly.
D) Teasing: Making fun of someone in a playful way

31

An **infant** is the stage of a human from birth to one-year-old where they need much attention and care since they couldn't do things on themselves yet.

Which of the following developments is greatly influenced by the ability of an infant to form healthy, secure attachments to caregivers?

A) Independence
B) Decision-making
C) Language acquisition
D) Social skills

CONTINUE ▶

32

Dating violence refers to abusive behavior such as physical, sexual, threats, or emotional aggression towards a romantic relationship.

Which of the following strategies can a health education program best help students in preventing teen dating violence?

A) Create a values subject that shows on what extent can behavior be considered abusive.

B) Create harsh punishments such as expulsion to students who will commit threats, unwanted physical contact, and harassment.

C) Help students, their families, and school staff discuss behaviors and social and cultural influences that can foster violence.

D) Let dating students learn forgiveness when one has committed abusive behavior.

33

Prosocial behavior refers to the voluntary behavior in helping others such as donating, sharing, giving gifts and obeying the rules.

Which of the following development closely links the growth of prosocial behavior toward peers in young children with ages between 5 and 8?

A) Explaining the long-term benefits and costs of interpersonal relationships

B) Opting to use nonverbal communication frequently

C) Having empathy for other people

D) Choosing people to deal with

CONTINUE ▶

34

Which of the following is the best choice of available fitness tests for a teacher to use to assess students with disabilities?

A) Brockport Physical Fitness Test
B) Basic Fitness test
C) Limited fitness activity
D) Fitnessgram

35

In a parents' meeting, Dina, a mother of three, shares about how open they are as a family. Each week, they decide a specific day, time and place where they can meet and talk about their whole week activities. Each of the family members has the chance to express his or her thoughts and even bothering thoughts entirely. In turn, family members will carefully listen and express their feelings and opinions.

Which of the following abilities does this practice affect each family member?

A) Protect each family member's feelings and ignore undeserving people.
B) Create consistent behavior towards each family member.
C) Develop effective problem-solving.
D) Firmly practice the family's strong arguments with other people.

36

Being a college student, you are trained to prepare the life of being professional and being away from home. David, a freshman student, was dropped off on his dormitory by his dad. Being away for the first time, David bid goodbye with a heavy heart to his father, but they both agreed to have electronic communication from time to time to update each other.

Which of the following best describes the benefit and value of this mediated communication?

A) Always having support in all areas especially finances
B) Maintaining an existing relationship during a transition period
C) Maximizing the use of technology
D) Scheduling frequent visitations to help in school requirements

37

A **gender role** refers to the accepted and appropriate behaviors that are culturally defined such as masculinity and femininity.

Which of the following typically exerts the most significant influence on the development of gender roles?

A) Judgments to people
B) Socialization process
C) Competency
D) Maslow's hierarchy of needs

38

On May 2016, a fire accident caused hundreds of families the loss of their homes, businesses, and investments. The incident had put their state on calamity where any donation would matter, and also psychological help was sought to help the families to cope with the tragedy.

Which of the following would be an effective strategy to help families overcome the situation and refresh their lives?

A) Determine the culprit who started the fire and let him or her pay for what he or she has done.

B) Collaborate on dealing with the immediate situation.

C) Transfer to nearby areas and ask them if they could let the families in until they could rebuild their homes.

D) Wait on donations to arrive.

39

Dino and Maria, a newlywed young couple, recently had a baby daughter named Ella, who is six months old.

As a young parent, which of the following skills must they learn to make appropriate parenting decisions?

A) Career

B) Social

C) Communication

D) Management

CONTINUE ▶

40

Peer mediation is the process of setting two or more students involved in a conflict meet in a confidential setting to solve their problems with the help of a trained student mediator.

Which of the following must students need to learn first in the peer mediation program or to manage their anger in conflict situations?

A) Exploring creative alternatives

B) Listening with care and respect

C) Strong rejection response

D) Finding someone to let out all the anger piled inside

41

The most common problem encountered in most characteristic of the primitive stage of forward rolling is due to which of the following problems?

A) The curl is lost

B) The chin is tucked

C) Head contact by hands

D) The knees and hips are flexed

42

Carbohydrate is any of a large group of organic compounds occurring in foods and living tissues and including sugars, starch, and cellulose.

Which of the following are the two main functions of carbohydrates in the body?

A) Build and repair body tissues
B) Provide energy for cells and maintaining an energy reserve
C) Synthesize and secrete complex fatty acid substances
D) Repair damaged cells and creating new ones

43

Which of the following best describes the effect of increasing rates of sedentary activity and poor dietary practices over rates of physical activities in adolescents?

A) Increase in stress-related disease
B) Increase in mineral-deficiency diseases
C) Increase in fatigue-related diseases
D) Increase in incidence of obesity-related diseases

44

The study shows strong and consistent evidence from observational studies that physical inactivity and poor fitness are associated with higher illness and death from all causes.

Which of the following diseases occurs mostly in people with poor fitness level and inactivity to physical activities?

A) Migraines
B) Fever and allergies
C) High blood pressure
D) Bacterial infection

45

Aerobic exercises are any of various sustained exercises such as jogging, rowing, swimming, or cycling that stimulate and strengthen the heart and lungs.

By doing regular aerobic exercises, which of the following is the best physiological adaptation in the body?

A) The maximum heartbeat increases
B) The heart can pump more blood throughout the body
C) The lungs are being filtered out of toxins to improve breathing
D) The body is better able to produce energy from fat stored as triglycerides

CONTINUE ▶

46

Which of the following improvements is experienced by people who do yoga according to the Mayo Clinic?

A) Production of testosterone, clearer eyesight, and younger looks

B) Healthier skin, digestive health, and more active

C) Becoming more fit, management of chronic conditions, and reduce stress

D) Faster thinking, increase in appetite, and clearer eyesight

47

In order to assess the skills of students during a basketball skills unit, which of the following would be the most appropriate way a teacher do?

A) Have them watch basketball games

B) Have them make an essay about basketball

C) Match two teams and watch which team will win

D) When moving through the unit, assess learners by developing a rubric

48

Diabetes is a group of metabolic disorders in which there are high blood sugar levels over a prolonged period.

Which of the following is the benefit of exercise on treatment plans of diabetic people?

A) Reduce the build-up of glucose in the blood
B) Prevent diabetes-induced changes in vision
C) Increase the production of insulin in the pancreas
D) Reduce body weight of diabetic people

49

A mother wants to determine what her 10-year-old child needs for bone growth and development.

Which of the following nutritional areas should be focused?

A) Adequate potassium intake
B) Adequate B-vitamins intake
C) Adequate fiber intake
D) Adequate calcium intake

50

Which of the following are the two principles of modern muscle strength and endurance conditioning followed by a person who lifted a newborn bull onto his shoulders each day until the bull became fully mature?

A) Overload and progression
B) Retention and stress
C) Progression and intensity
D) Strength and variable resistance

51

Total daily calorie needs are the number of calories need to maintain per day.

Which of the following stages of growth and development is the highest amount of total daily calorie needs?

A) Late adulthood
B) Early adulthood
C) Infancy
D) Adolescence

CONTINUE ▶

52

Rico's daily intake, as well as his daily expenditure of calories, is 3,000. Judith has 3,000 daily intakes of calories while she has a daily expenditure of calories of 2,000. Timothy has a calorie daily intake of 2,000 and a daily expenditure of 2,800 calories. Lastly, Aliana has a daily intake of 1,000 calories and a daily expenditure of 4,000 calories.

Who among the four persons would most likely to lose weight safely?

A) Aliana
B) Timothy
C) Judith
D) Rico

53

Cooling down is an easy exercise, done after a more intense activity, to allow the body to gradually transition to a resting or near-resting state while stretching is a form of physical exercise in which a specific muscle or tendon is deliberately flexed.

Which of the following is the benefit of doing cool-down and stretching activities after strenuous cardiorespiratory fitness activities?

A) Prevent an abrupt decrease in the glucose level
B) Prevent the reduction of carbohydrates and fat composition in the body
C) Prevent muscle soreness and blood pooling in the extremities
D) Trigger a final surge in metabolic rate before the body reverts to a resting state

54

Why does the warm-up period before exercise help in preserving the joints?

A) Because it increases the proportion of blood in the thoracic cavity.
B) Becuase it stimulates the release of synovial fluid, which lubricates the joints.
C) Because it activates the sympathetic nervous system.
D) Because it encourages the uptake of lactic acid.

55

Which of the following about the Society of Health and Physical Educators (SHAPE AMERICA) is not correct?

A) Its mission is to enhance knowledge; improve professional practice; and increase support for high-quality physical education.
B) It provides programs and resources to support health and physical educators at every level.
C) American Alliance for Health and Recreation and Dance (AAHPERD) were previously given names of it.
D) It has been founded in 1985 and it is a membership organization of health and physical education professionals.

56

In order to learn a new takedown technique, which of the following technology applications would best support a wrestler?

A) Gathering information from co-wrestlers
B) Proper execution of viewed pictures on a video screen
C) Reading about the proper technique and procedure on the internet
D) Watching other wrestler's performance

57

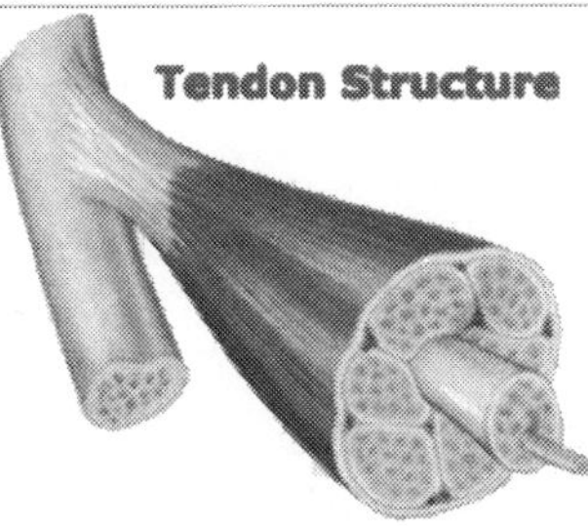

Tendon is a flexible but inelastic cord of strong fibrous collagen tissue.

Which of the following is the main function of tendons in the skeletal system?

A) Attach bones to muscles
B) Attach bones to other bones
C) Attach ligaments to muscle fibers
D) Act as the source of calcium phosphate

58

On athlete's sports performance, a primary short-term effect of amphetamines is illustrated by which of the following?

A) The risk of injury decreases
B) Feelings of alertness increases
C) Thinking process decreases
D) The growth of muscles increases

59

A risk factor is something that increases your chance of getting a disease.

Which of the following modifiable risk factors are associated with coronary artery disease according to the American Heart Association?

A) Age and ethnic background
B) Stress and physical inactivity
C) Age and family history
D) Smoking and alcohol consumption

CONTINUE ▶

60

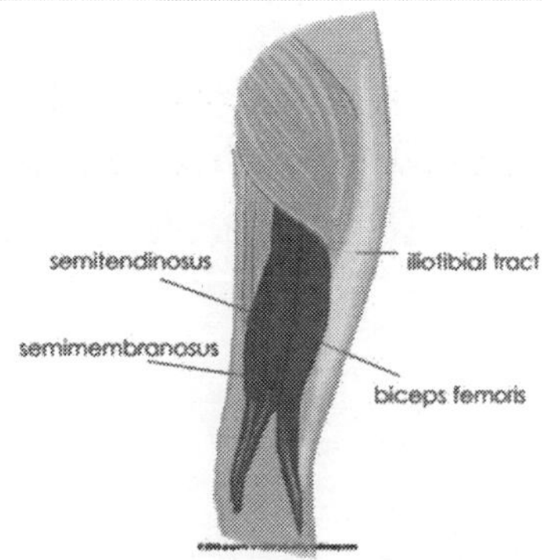

The hamstring muscle group consists of three separate muscles; the semitendinosus, semimembranosus and biceps femoris. They originate from the lower part of the pelvis and insert into the back of the shin bone. When contracting they mainly bend the knee and extend the hip joint.

One of your students has been strained in his hamstring muscle. Which of the following pieces would be the proper treatment?

A) Applying ice and compressing the leg
B) Applying ice and stretching the leg
C) Applying heat and compressing the leg
D) Applying heat and stretching the leg

61

In order for a physical education teacher to complete and adhere to at the beginning of the school year in an effort to establish good classroom management, which of the following sets of tasks would be the best?

A) Learning the basics of an activity
B) Make posters for announcements
C) Letting the students do fitness tests whenever they want
D) Having an organized system of rules, records, lesson with the participation of students

CONTINUE ▶

62

The fitness program is a plan to help someone improve their health and physical condition.

Which of the following sets of health-related components is emphasized in a personal fitness program that performs appropriate stretching exercises during warmup and cool-down for both jogging and weight lifting, jogging 3 days a week for 30–45 minutes and lifting weights 3 days a week?

A) Cardiorespiratory endurance, muscular strength, and flexibility

B) Cardiorespiratory endurance, body composition, and flexibility

C) Cardiorespiratory endurance, muscular strength, and agility

D) Cardiorespiratory endurance, agility, and flexibility

63

Which of the following should be emphasized to children to have healthy eating practices and patterns?

A) Stimulate growth hormone production faster

B) Increase endurance and stamina without exercise

C) Reduce time for sleep to have more play time

D) Help prevent both short- and long-term health problems such as colds, dental cavities, and obesity

64

The linear relationship between the physiological factor and oxygen consumption is shown in which of the following lists?

A) Red blood cell count, blood type, respiration rate

B) Work rate, heart rate, cardiac rate

C) Blood pressure, work rate, minute ventilation

D) Pulse rate, red blood cell count, core temperature

65

Body composition is used to describe the percentages of fat, bone, water, and muscle in bodies.

Which of the following is the main concern of body composition as a component of health-related fitness?

A) Muscle formation in the body

B) Relative proportions of fat and lean tissue in the body

C) The relative amount of vitamins present in the body

D) Maintenance of bone mass in the body

CONTINUE ▶

66

Cross-training refers to combining exercises of other disciplines, different than that of the athlete in training. Swimming and jogging could be an example of cross-training activities.

Which of the following is the best physiological change in the body after weeks of doing cross-training activities?

A) Increased weight of muscles
B) Improved bone mass and strength
C) Improved ratio of high-density lipoproteins (HDLs) to low-density lipoproteins (LDLs)
D) Increased length of long bones and decreased length of tendons attached to long bones

67

In physical education class, the maximum heart rate that should characterize students' exercise for health-related fitness is best expressed by which of the following heart rate percentage?

A) A maximum heart rate of 10-35%
B) A maximum heart rate of 35-60%
C) A maximum heart rate of 60-85%
D) A maximum heart rate of 85-95%

68

Standing toe touch is bending at the waist, keeping your legs straight until you can relax and let your upper body hang down in front of you. Let your arms and hands hang down naturally.

Which of the following is the main reason that a straight-legged standing toe-touch is a high-risk exercise?

A) Maximizes hamstring stretch reflex
B) Elongates cervical ligaments causing muscle sore
C) Increases pressure on lumbar disks and overstretch lumbar ligaments
D) Uses the latissimus dorsi as a shoulder extensor, which hyper-extends the shoulders.

69

After every vigorous physical activity, cooling -down is performed.

Which of the following is not an immediate physiological benefit of cool-down?

A) Cooldown promotes the reduction of cholesterol in the blood
B) Cooldown prevents blood from pooling in the legs
C) Cooldown reduces the risk of cardiac irregularities
D) Cooldown increases the rate of lactic acid removal from the blood and skeletal muscle

70

Nutrition is the process of providing or obtaining the food necessary for health and growth.

To promote optimum growth and development in young children, which of the following is the suggested nutritional practice?

A) Consuming high dietary fiber for good digestion
B) Consuming more protein to aid in developing more muscles
C) Consuming more fatty foods to increase stored energy
D) Consuming three moderately large meals and avoiding or limiting snacks and treats to promote desirable eating patterns

71

Negligence is a term that means carelessness or a breach of an obligation.

In case of a student acquiring injury in a physical education class, which of the following teaching practices will protect the teacher from possible charges of negligence?

A) Doing group feedback discussions than individual evaluation
B) Allowing students not to participate in activities they are not fine doing
C) Providing students with developmentally-appropriate instruction based on recommended skills progressions
D) Ensuring that the students always have a written copy of instructions

72

Cardiopulmonary resuscitation (CPR) is a lifesaving technique useful in many emergencies, including heart attack or near drowning.

Which of the following is the main purpose of rescue breathing and chest compressions in doing CPR?

A) Produce electric shock to retrieve heart rhythm

B) Remove any object trapped inside the heart

C) Provide artificial ventilation for a victim who is in severe respiratory distress

D) Oxygenate and circulate the blood in a victim whose heart has stopped beating

SECTION 2 - HEALTH EDUCATION

#	Answer	Topic	Subtopic	#	Answer	Topic	Subtopic	#	Answer	Topic	Subtopic	#	Answer	Topic	Subtopic
1	A	TA	S3	19	B	TA	S3	37	B	TA	S3	55	D	TA	S2
2	B	TA	S1	20	A	TA	S1	38	B	TA	S3	56	B	TA	S2
3	B	TA	S1	21	C	TA	S3	39	C	TA	S3	57	A	TA	S1
4	D	TA	S1	22	A	TA	S3	40	B	TA	S3	58	B	TA	S1
5	A	TA	S3	23	D	TA	S3	41	A	TA	S1	59	B	TA	S2
6	A	TA	S3	24	C	TA	S1	42	B	TA	S1	60	A	TA	S2
7	D	TA	S3	25	C	TA	S2	43	D	TA	S1	61	D	TA	S2
8	D	TA	S1	26	D	TA	S3	44	C	TA	S1	62	A	TA	S2
9	A	TA	S3	27	A	TA	S3	45	D	TA	S1	63	D	TA	S2
10	A	TA	S1	28	B	TA	S1	46	C	TA	S1	64	D	TA	S1
11	B	TA	S2	29	C	TA	S3	47	D	TA	S2	65	B	TA	S1
12	A	TA	S3	30	A	TA	S3	48	A	TA	S2	66	C	TA	S1
13	D	TA	S3	31	D	TA	S3	49	D	TA	S1	67	C	TA	S2
14	D	TA	S3	32	C	TA	S3	50	A	TA	S1	68	C	TA	S2
15	A	TA	S3	33	C	TA	S3	51	D	TA	S2	69	A	TA	S1
16	A	TA	S3	34	A	TA	S2	52	B	TA	S2	70	D	TA	S2
17	A	TA	S3	35	C	TA	S3	53	C	TA	S2	71	C	TA	S2
18	C	TA	S3	36	B	TA	S3	54	B	TA	S1	72	D	TA	S1

Topics & Subtopics

Code	Description	Code	Description
SA1	Health Knowledge	SA3	Healthy Interpersonal Relationships
SA2	Health Instruction	TA	Health Education

CONTINUE ▶

TEST DIRECTION

DIRECTIONS

Read the questions carefully and then choose the ONE best answer to each question.

Be sure to allocate your time carefully so you are able to complete the entire test within the testing session. You may go back and review your answers at any time.

You may use any available space in your test booklet for scratch work.

Questions in this booklet are not actual test questions but they are the samples for commonly asked questions.

This test aims to cover all topics which may appear on the actual test. However some topics may not be covered.

Studying this booklet will be preparing you for the actual test. It will not guarantee improving your test score but it will help you pass your exam on the first attempt.

Some useful tips for answering multiple choice questions;

- Start with the questions that you can easily answer.

- Underline the keywords in the question.

- Be sure to read all the choices given.

- Watch for keywords such as NOT, always, only, all, never, completely.

- Do not forget to answer every question.

CONTINUE ▶

1

Movement is powered by skeletal muscles, which are attached to the skeleton at various sites on bones. Muscles, bones, and joints provide the principal mechanics for movement, all coordinated by the nervous system.

Which of the following about the skeletal system is not correct?

A) Osteoporosis is a disease that causes bones to become weak and brittle.

B) A tendon is a fibrous connective tissue which attaches muscle to muscle.

C) Arthritis is a disorder of the joints. It involves inflammation of one or more joints.

D) Joints are structures where two bones are attached. A ligament is the fibrous connective tissue that connects bones to other bones.

2

Cooling down is an easy exercise, done after more intense activity, to allow the body to gradually rest.

Which of the following about cooling down is not correct?

A) It allows the heart rate to return to its resting rate.

B) A simple and effective means of cooling down is to continue to exercise at a slower pace.

C) It provides the body with a quick transition from exercise back to a steady state of rest.

D) Cooling down after physical activity is important because it prevents muscle soreness.

CONTINUE ▶

3

Rubella is a viral infection known for its characteristic red rash. Although considered a relatively mild disease, it can pose a serious threat to several people.

Which of the following is the most critical reason for immunization against rubella?

A) A person infected by rubella can develop a case of meningitis or encephalitis that can result in death.

B) An elderly adult who incurred rubella as a child is at risk of acquiring a painful and debilitating case of shingles.

C) A pregnant woman who incurs rubella during the first trimester of her pregnancy can give birth to an infant with severe congenital disabilities.

D) A baby who contracts rubella is at risk of permanent paralysis resulting from nervous and muscular degradation in the arms and legs.

4

According to health experts, when an individual has a small chance of acting on its own, he or she may acquire a deep-seated need for control.

Once this need is achieved through excessive control over one's body, it becomes a coping response that is vital in the development of which of the following disorders?

A) Anorexia or bulimia nervosa

B) Asperger's syndrome

C) Bipolar or manic-depressive disorder

D) Schizophrenia

5

Fitness can be defined as the condition of being physically fit and healthy. Which of the following about the fitness is not correct?

A) The primary advantage of health-related physical fitness is to improve muscle strength.

B) The more you sweat during a workout, the more fat the body is burning" is not true. "No pain, no gain" is a workout myth.

C) Fitness is not merely the absence of disease or infirmity but it is a form of physical activity done primarily to improve one's health and physical fitness.

D) Maintaining physical fitness does not require major lifestyle changes. Fitness can be achieved through small changes in what you eat and your level of activity.

CONTINUE ▶

6

In the last 20 years, there has been an increase in Type 2 diabetes.

Which of the following is the primary cause of this event?

A) The increase in adults and children having unhealthy diet and bad exercise habits.
B) The increase in individuals from the population susceptible to Type 2 diabetes.
C) The increase in adults having substance abuse.
D) The increase in the survival rates of people with diabetes.

7

Tertiary Prevention's goal is to slow the progression of diseases and reduce the complications.

Which of the following about tertiary prevention is not correct?

A) Tertiary prevention aims to detect a disease in its earliest stages, before symptoms appear.
B) The treatments of tertiary prevention can include several professionals including doctor, medical specialist, occupational therapist, physiotherapist and etc.
C) Helping people handle complex health problems and injuries to improve quality of life and their life expectancy is a goal of tertiary prevention.
D) Tertiary prevention refers to treating the disease like arthritis, asthma, heart disease, cancer and diabetes and providing rehabilitation for people who are already affected by a disease.

CONTINUE ▶

8

Which of the following term is not defined correctly?

A) Pathology is the study of the cause of disease

B) Life expectqncy is from birth, how long you are expected to live.

C) Total number of disease cases in a population is called as Prevalence

D) Morbidity is a public health term to describe the frequency of deaths produced by a disease or other condition

9

Consuming large amounts of foods and drinks containing sugar can cause various health problems on children such as obesity. Aside from sugar, adding phosphorous to a soda can also be harmful to children's health.

Which of the following is most likely the reason for this?

A) Calcium is drawn out of bones that are still developing since phosphorus binds with calcium.

B) The metabolism of fat-soluble vitamins is prevented by phosphorus.

C) Compared with adult kidneys, phosphorus can remain in a child's immature kidneys.

D) Formation of new cells with the help of water-soluble vitamins can be interfered by phosphorus.

CONTINUE ▶

10

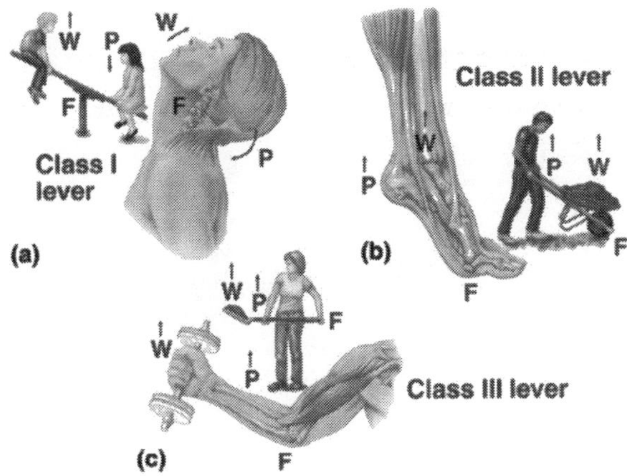

During physical training, your muscles do their job by pulling on your bones, which function as levers to create movement. First, second and third-class lever are the classifications of levers concerning physical exercises. The third-class lever is the most commonly used exercise in the body, but some use the first and second-class lever.

In the exercises shown below, which of the following involves the first-class lever?

A) Biceps curls
B) Triceps pushdown
C) Seated leg extensions
D) Push-ups

11

Which of the following agencies is responsible for the approval of using azidothymidine (AZT) as the treatment for AIDS?

A) Division of Consumer Affairs
B) Federal Trade Commission
C) Food and Drug Administration
D) Consumer Products Safety Commission

12

Warm-up is the preparation for a physical activity by exercising or practicing gently beforehand. Each workout should begin with a warm-up. A warm-up includes 4-5 minutes of slow jogging or walking. Warming up helps avoid injury.

Which of the following about warm-up is not correct?

A) A proper warm-up should raise your body temperature by one or two degrees Celsius.
B) It is very important that you stretch before the general warm-up.
C) Jogging slowly before running is a good warm-up because it will warm the muscles and increase the heart rate.
D) Once the general warm-up has been completed, the muscles will be more elastic and it will help reduce this risk of injury.

CONTINUE ▶

13

Which of the following best describes the shared function of the nervous system and the endocrine system?

A) To regulate the communication within the body
B) To activate the reproductive glands
C) To control the balance of blood pressure and water in the body
D) To regulate the development and growth.

14

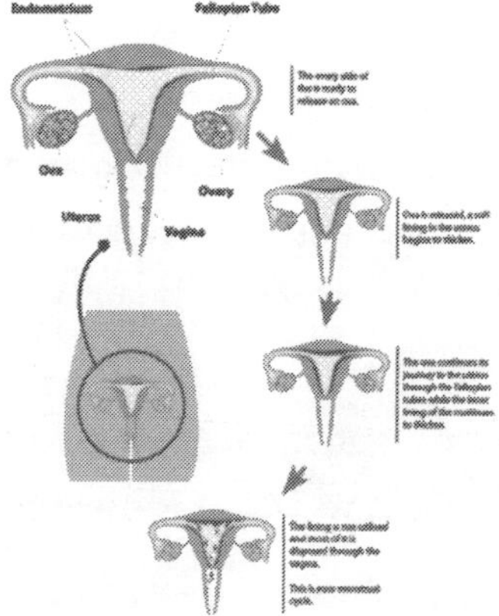

Every month, a woman's body undergoes a hormonal process, known as the **menstrual cycle**, for the preparation of a possible pregnancy.

On average, how many days does the ovulation phase of the menstrual cycle happen?

A) 7 to 10 days
B) 28 to 30 days
C) 3 to 5 days
D) 14 to 15 days

15

A **prescription** is an order that tells the pharmacist what medication is needed for the patient.

For which of the following you would most likely need to get a prescription from a doctor?

A) Diet Pills
B) Analgesics
C) Vitamin supplements
D) Birth control pills

16

Violence prevention programs should be established between which of the following?

A) School, Home and Community
B) School and County
C) School, Home and State
D) Home and District

17

Children need to have good healthy eating patterns to avoid any future health problems.

Which of the following methods would most likely be effective in motivating children to practice healthy eating patterns?

A) Fruit beverages are given to them instead of raw or cooked vegetables and fruits.
B) Foods that are refined or processed are avoided.
C) Candies or anything sweet is offered as a reward upon completing a balanced meal.
D) Foods from all the major groups of food are included in their meals.

18

Accidental injuries are one of the most frequent causes of death in children.

Which of the following is the most significant risk factor for injuries among children?

A) Lack of education
B) Living in poverty
C) Accident susceptibility
D) Lack of parental supervision

19

The process involving changes in the physical appearance as a child's body undergoes maturity into an adult body is called **puberty**.

In males, which of the following occurs first during puberty?

A) The appearance of facial hair
B) Changes in the voice
C) Increase in the size of the testes
D) Shoulder widening

20

Human actions towards the environment have advantages and disadvantages. One an example of its disadvantages is acid rain.

Which of the following human activities is the primary source of acid rain?

A) The burning of solid wastes.
B) Use of wood stoves for heating homes.
C) Fossil fuels being incenerated in smelters, mills, and power plants.
D) The use of substances in manufacturing that emit radiation.

21

Endurance is the ability of an organism to remain active for a long period of time. **Muscular endurance** is the ability of a muscle or group of muscles to sustain repeated contractions against a resistance for a long period of time. It is one of the components of muscular fitness, along with muscular strength and power.

Which of the following about muscular endurance is not correct?

A) Muscular endurance is not related to a person's muscular strength.

B) Improving your muscular endurance can make everyday activities easier.

C) The combination of strength and endurance results in muscular endurance.

D) To be able to run quickly over a short distance is an example of muscular endurance.

22

The immune system is the defense system of the body that contains cells categorized as lymphocytes, monocytes, and neutrophils.

In which of the following do these cells move throughout the body?

A) The nutrients of the digestive system

B) The fluids of the circulatory and lymphatic systems

C) The neurotransmitters of the nervous system

D) The hormones of the reproductive and endocrine systems

23

Several studies show that lack of sleep is correlatead with diabetes, heart disease, immune system suppression.

Which of the following groups is at most risk of having the mentioned health concerns?

A) Employees working atleast 40 hours per week
B) Student working atleast 20 hours per week
C) Low socioeconomic status groups
D) High socioeconomic status groups

24

Which of the following statements best describes the essential amino acids?

A) These are the amino acids considered as high-energy nutrients for promoting growth and development.
B) These are important constituents of fats, carbohydrates, and proteins.
C) These are the amino acids that occur naturally and are primarily responsible for fighting infections.
D) These are the amino acids needed for the synthesis of proteins but mostly cannot be produced by the body.

25

When lead builds up in the body, **lead poisoning** occurs and it can cause serious health problems.

Which of the following in older dwellings can be one of the reasons of lead poisoning?

A) Insulation materials on the walls.
B) Paint on the walls and woodwork.
C) Frayed electrical wirings and switches.
D) Corroded pipes and channels of heating and cooling systems.

26

Exercise is often described as training and exertion of the lungs, muscles, and heart. Even moderate exercise reduces the risk of heart disease, diabetes, hypertension, and obesity because exercise is the silver bullet for a better quality of life.

Which of the following about the exercise is not correct?

A) Frequency, duration, intensity, and kind of exercises are important points to consider for a desirable level of fitness.

B) Exercise reduces the risk of diabetes and cardiac injury during a heart attack. It also increases bone mass.

C) Exercise is one of several components of a lifestyle that leads to wellness. Weight loss should be the main reason for people to exercise.

D) There are plenty of exercises you can do at home or outdoors using your own body weight and gravity. Some examples include jumping jacks, push-ups, and sit-ups.

27

The cholesterol content of baked desserts can be manipulated by modifying certain ingredients.

Among the ingredients commonly used in baking, which of the following can reduce cholesterol content effectively?

A) Using egg whites instead of whole eggs.

B) Using raw sugar instead of refined sugar.

C) Using shortening instead of cooking oil.

D) Using all-purpose flour instead of whole wheat flour.

CONTINUE ▶

28

Human development is a lifetime process of change. Throughout this procedure, an individual acquires values and attitudes that supervise understanding, choices, and relationships.

According to studies, which of the following factors has the most substantial positive impact on the emotional health and wellness of older adults?

A) Taking care of grandchildren or any other young relative.

B) Trying different lifestyles and self-refining activities.

C) Maintaining closer ties with family and friends.

D) Working full time until past the usual well passed retirement age range.

29

Which of the following about the minerals is not correct?

A) Exposure to Chromium VI causes the highest risk of cancer.

B) Calcium, potassium, and sodium are classified as Catecholamines.

C) Iodine deficiency can result in permanent mental retardation.

D) Minerals are the nutrients from the soil that are found in foods.

30

Which of the following statements best describes cardiorespiratory fitness?

A) It is the ability to create force constantly without feeling exhausted.

B) It is the ability to execute aerobic activity for an extended time.

C) It is the ability to do repetitive high-intensity muscle contractions.

D) It is the ability to perform vigorous physical activity without experiencing discomfort or stiffness.

31

Several factors affect a person's development concerning physical health and nutritional habits. These factors may be positive or negative.

Which of the following would have the most significant positive influence on such?

A) Gathering information about the benefits of exercise from sources like magazine articles.

B) Gaining knowledge about food preparation from watching cooking shows.

C) Joining extracurricular activities after school or work.

D) Being exposed in an environment that practices and values health habits.

32

Complex carbohydrates consist of a long and complex chain of sugar molecules andthey are larger than a simple carbohydrate.

Which of the following is the reason that endurance athletes view complex carbohydrates as an excellent source of energy?

A) An immediate and a timed-release energy source can be provided by complex carbohydrates since they can easily be digested.

B) Complex carbohydrates cannot be depleted from muscles by intense exercise since they are slow to metabolize.

C) The liver can convert complex carbohydrates into triglycerides that are stored throughout the body.

D) Athletes will not easily feel hunger since complex carbohydrates induce a feeling of fullness without adding extra calories.

33

Health is a dynamic state of complete physical, mental, and social well-being. It is not only the absence of disease or infirmity. On the other hand, **Public Health** is the science of protecting and improving the health of individuals and their communities.

Which of the following about public health is not correct?

A) Public health refers to what the society does to help the people to be healthy.

B) The primary goal of public health is to help and cure infected people.

C) Public Health Promotion targets the entire population and aims to improve overall health.

D) Assessment, policy development, and assurance are the critical functions of public health.

34

Which of the following is not one of the benefits of physical activity?

A) Social benefit; physical activity can help develop friendships.

B) Physical benefit; physical activity can help to relieve tension and contributes to weight loss.

C) Mental benefit; physical activity improves blood glucose control in type 2 diabetes.

D) Health benefit; regular physical activity can prevent high blood pressure, help arthritis.

35

Athletes tend to drink more water because it helps regulate body temperature and lubricate the joints. Water also helps deliver the necessary nutrients to the body to gain energy. However, consuming too much water, or over-hydration, can dilute the sodium levels of the body.

Which of the following describes this type of condition?

A) Hypothermia
B) Hyperthermia
C) Hyponatremia
D) Hypernatremia

36

Which of the following does a family (the building block of the society) system contribute to?

A) Provide developmental experiences for all members.
B) Provide a stable physical environment for all members.
C) Meet physical and emotional needs of individuals.
D) Meet educational and social needs of individuals.

37

Which of the following minerals should adolescents that reached puberty, need to increase their intake compared with prepubescent girls?

A) Zinc (Zn)
B) Phosphorus (Ph)
C) Iron (Fe)
D) Iodine (I)

38

Haemophilus influenzae type b (Hib) may cause a life-threatening infection that can lead to severe disease, especially in children. Which of the following defines it best?

A) Fungal infection
B) Viral infection
C) Bacterial infection
D) Immune disease

CONTINUE ▶

39

Human immunodeficiency virus or **HIV** is a microorganism that targets the immune system of the body, making a person more susceptible to diseases.

Which of the following is a vital risk factor for incurring HIV among sexually active people?

A) Getting an organ transplant or blood transmission
B) Having a concealed hereditary blood disease
C) Being frequently involved in kissing with different people
D) Being sexually engaged to a person with multiple partners

40

Fungal diseases, like athlete's foot and ringworms, are prevented by which of the following?

A) Maintaining a balanced diet and exercising regularly
B) Washing hands carefully and avoiding direct contact with infected people
C) Cooking animal food thoroughly and avoiding contaminated water
D) Practicing good personal hygiene and using dry clothes

41

The CDC or the Centers for Disease Control and Prevention is a national health facility that aims to preserve public health and security through the control and prevention of disease, injury, and disability.

According to CDC, which of the following is included in the top five causes of death for people aged 15 to 19?

A) Unintentional injuries
B) Anemia
C) Pneumonia
D) Diabetes

CONTINUE ▶

42

Insomnia is a disease which is also known as sleeplessness. It is a sleep disorder which is caused by psychiatric and medical conditions, unhealthy sleep habits, specific substances, and certain biological factors that makes it difficult to fall asleep.

People with sleeplessness can have difficulty falling asleep, waking up often during the night and having trouble going back to sleep again.

Which of the following stress management techniques would be effective for an individual suffering from insomnia?

A) An exercise program
B) Progressive relaxation
C) Stress inoculation
D) Guided imagery

43

Aerobics is the energetic physical exercises that make the heart, lungs, and muscles stronger, It increases the amount of oxygen in the blood.

Which of the following about aerobic exercise, which is also known as cardio, is not correct?

A) Aerobics is best for improving cardiovascular health.
B) Anaerobic exercise is last-lasting, low-intensity activity.
C) Aerobic exercise promotes circulation throughout the blood.
D) Aerobics is an appropriate method of training to improve your flexibility.

CONTINUE ▶

44

In 1928, Alexander Fleming, a Professor of Bacteriology at St. Mary's Hospital in London, accidentally discovered penicillin. **Penicillins** are a group of drugs that attack a wide variety of bacteria by interfering with the bacterial cell walls.

Which of the following diseases is treated by using penicillin?

A) Athlete's Foot: A fungal infection, also called tinea pedis, that usually begins between the toes.

B) Pneumonia: A respiratory infection that inflames the air sacs in one or both lungs.

C) Genital Herpes: A common, highly contagious sexually transmitted disease (STD) caused by infection by the herpes simplex virus type 2 (HSV-2).

D) Trichinosis: An infection caused by the roundworm Trichinella spiralis or another Trichinella species.

45

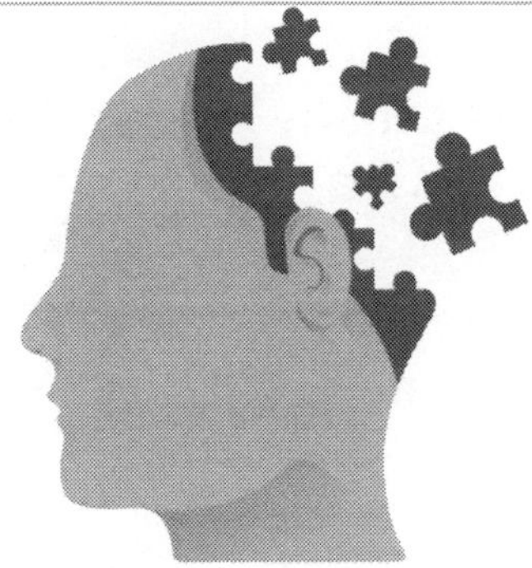

Alzheimer's disease is an irreversible, chronic brain disorder that slowly destroys thinking and memory skills, and eventually the ability to do the simplest tasks. It is the most common cause of dementia among adults.

Which of the following is considered a risk factor linked with the onset of Alzheimer'sEarly retirement disease?

A) Lack of exercise

B) Gain of weight

C) Early retirement

D) High consumption of green vegetables

CONTINUE ▶

46

Schizophrenia is a long-term mental condition that affects how a person thinks, feels, and behaves. People with schizophrenia may seem like they have lost touch with reality.

At which of the following age brackets are people most likely diagnosed with schizophrenia?

A) Around college age
B) As a child
C) During adolescence
D) In older adulthood

47

The ecosystem can be preserved optimally by which of the following scenarios shown below?

A) The non-living components of the ecosystem are regarded as not important and replaceable; unlike the living components, the plants and animals, which are protected.
B) The alteration of the ecosystem's territorial space only.
C) Obtaining natural resources from the ecosystem at a rate which will support human needs.
D) Recycling and reusing all resources and maintaining the energy level within the ecosystem constant.

48

Sexual assault is a kind of sexual violence wherein a person intentionally touches another person without permission or persuades or physically forces a person to engage in a sexual act against their will.

Which of the following statements would be the most practical approach to promote the students' capability to protect themselves from sexual assault?

A) Improving and giving separate lessons for boys and girls based on statistical facts associated with sexual assaults by gender.

B) Implementing lessons on self-defense techniques and martial arts skills through physical education or community events

C) Introducing studies collected by law enforcement agencies on the strategies of sexual predators

D) Nourishing the students' knowledge of principles and techniques for understanding risky circumstances

49

Primary prevention focuses on good populations, and it is implemented before disease occurs.

Which of the following about primary prevention is not correct?

A) Primary prevention aims to prevent disease or health problems before exposure or onset of illness.

B) Immunization is an example of primary prevention, and the primary objective of immunization programs is to cure the infection.

C) Law enforcement to ban or control the use of unhealthy or hazardous products is an example of primary prevention.

D) Education about healthy and safe habits, altering unhealthy or unsafe behaviors that can lead to disease or injury is an example of primary prevention.

CONTINUE ▶

50

What biomolecule is converted into glucose by muscle cells which is also a multi-branched polysaccharide of glucose that serves as a storage of energy in animals, fungi, and humans?

A) Muscle glycogen
B) High triglycerides
C) Free fatty acids
D) Creatine phosphate

51

Cardiovascular endurance is how efficiently your heart, blood vessels, and lungs to supply oxygen-rich blood to working muscles during physical activity for more than 90 seconds.

Which of the following about cardiovascular endurance is not correct?

A) Cardiorespiratory endurance is also known as aerobic fitness.
B) Cardiovascular endurance can not be negatively affected by heart disease.
C) The Cooper 12 minute run test is a suitable method for measuring your cardiovascular endurance.
D) Cardiorespiratory endurance is usually measured in terms of maximum oxygen uptake

52

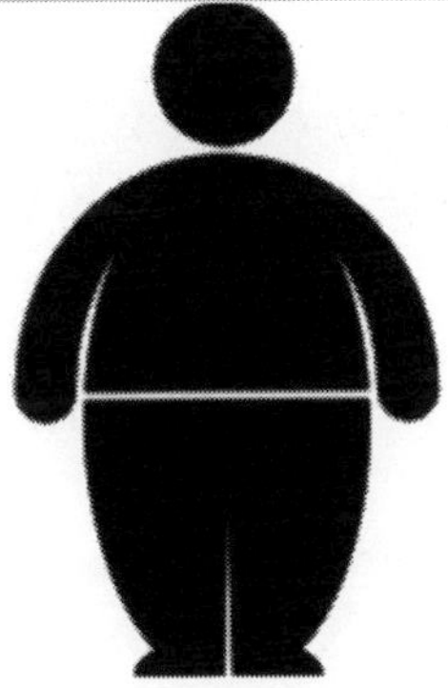

One way to measure the body's readiness for exercise is to use the **body mass index (BMI)** measurement. BMI is a person's weight in kilograms (kg) divided by his or her height in meters squared. It can be used to screen for weight categories that may lead to health problems but it is not diagnostic of the body fatness or health of an individual.

Which one of the following is the BMI score that indicates obesity?

A) 14
B) 22
C) 26
D) 31

53

A girl is attempting to build a Barbie House out of legos. After several barbie houses fall over, the girl moves along to play with a Barbie Baby.

Which of the following internal ability does this behavior reflect?

A) Playing with a variety of toys
B) Modifying emotional responses
C) Determining learning strengths
D) Continuing with a task under pressure

54

Children are more susceptive to different types of diseases, such as measles, tetanus, chicken pox, polio, and diphtheria because their organ systems are still developing.

Which of the following statements is a common characteristic of the diseases mentioned above?

A) All diseases have a significant impact on the immune system.
B) All diseases can be prevented by using vaccines.
C) All diseases are caused by bacteria.
D) All diseases affect the circulatory system.

55

Local departments of public health have very important responsibilities. Which of the following is one of these responsibilities?

A) Training interested community members in emergency first aid.
B) Organizing information about the infectious diseases within the community.
C) Administering physical fitness assessments of public school students.
D) Taking actions to ban unsafe health-related products which are sold in local stores.

56

Fear is the body's natural response to immediate danger, **anxiety** is a feeling of nervousness, or worry that generally occurs in the absence of an impending threat. Anxiety is a natural reaction to stress, so it can be helpful at times by making you more alert and ready for action.

Which of the following personal strategies would be the most effective for mitigating feelings of generalized anxiety and stress?

A) Ignoring distressing things in life hoping that they will end.
B) Expressing thoughts to a friend or family member frequently.
C) Redirecting attention and energy to a pleasant activity such as playing a game.
D) Challenging to tackle a difficult task that has been avoided before.

57

The fitness training principle of progressive overload is best illustrated in which of the following personal fitness plan situations?

A) Doing a more varied exercise routine
B) Slowly raising the strength or duration of exercise sessions
C) Trying different time spans between exercise sessions
D) Always allowing little or no rest between exercise sessions

58

Which of the following minerals are young children and women aged 20 to 35 years old most likely be deficient of?

A) Calcium (Ca)
B) Sodium (Na)
C) Potassium (K)
D) Iron (Fe)

CONTINUE ▶

59

Which of the following is the most likely reason why the effects of air pollution and soil contamination from pesticides usually does not manifest in a short term?

A) It affects the animal population first, rather than the human population.

B) Its clean up can be done quickly and effectively.

C) Avoiding exposure on such hazards is easy.

D) Its impact on health tend to develop slowly over time.

60

Health, as defined by the World Health Organization (WHO), is "a state of complete physical, mental and social well-being, and not merely the absence of disease or infirmity. Good health is achieving a balance of physical, spiritual, emotional, social, intellectual, and physical health.

Which of the following terms about health-related physical fitness is not defined correctly?

A) Agility is the ability to move quickly and easily, get a quick start and leave the opposition behind.

B) Strength is a physical fitness component that can also help in following a healthy lifestyle.

C) Flexibility is the ability to increase the range of movements possible at a joint and hold a better technical shape.

D) Coordination is the ability to stay in control of body movement, and balance is the ability to move two or more body parts under control, smoothly and efficiently.

CONTINUE ▶

61

Marga, after receiving a clean health bill from both her doctor and dentist, was instructed to have regularly scheduled check-ups, both medical and dental.

Which of the following statements best describes the reason for this?

A) If there are any injuries sustained during daily exercise routines, these injuries can be treated immediately, and not escalate any further.
B) To prevent an increase in the cost of her health insurance premiums.
C) To monitor her gain of weight to prevent her from becoming obese.
D) To detect any health problems that are developing to prevent it from advancing any further.

62

Which of the following is the reason why adolescents that experienced growth are physically uncoordinated?

A) Changes in the middle ear that occur late in adolescence is usually associated with the development of kinesthetic sense.
B) Fast fluctuations in metabolic processes result from the hormonal imbalances due to puberty.
C) The fast growth of the brain and the nervous system causes a lack of focus and concentration.
D) Growth rate of different parts of the musculoskeletal system are a different.

63

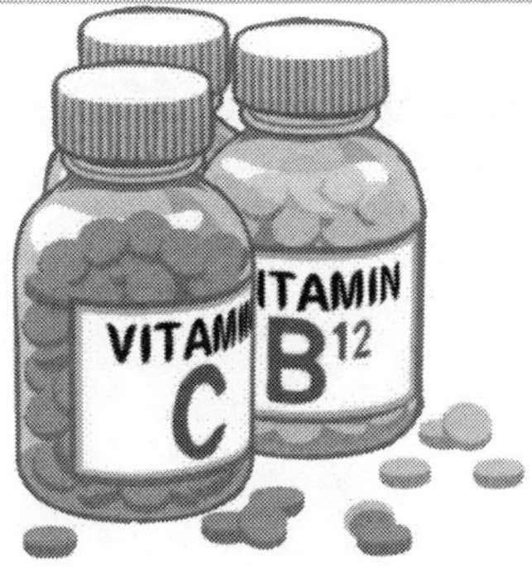

In the United States market, some public policies require the manufacturers to add vitamins and minerals on cereals and milk that are sold.

Which of the following is the primary purpose of this public policies?

A) To minimize the development of food intolerance conditions.

B) To increase the food product's nutrient value.

C) To protect the public from illnesses that can be derived from food

D) To extend the shelf life of food products.

64

Health-related physical fitness is made up of five components. The components of health-related physical fitness are muscular strength, muscular endurance, flexibility, cardiorespiratory endurance, and body composition.

Which of the following about health-related physical fitness and activities is not correct?

A) Females are less likely to show high skill levels in physical activities.

B) When beginning a new fitness routine some muscle aches and pains are not normal.

C) A lack of confidence is often given as a reason for non-participation in physical activities.

D) Watching an Olympic athlete and joining an athletics' club is the best example of a role model promoting participation in physical activities.

65

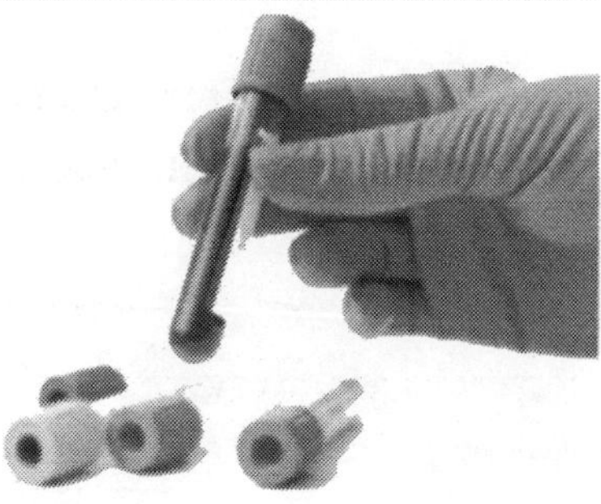

Blood screening is done to detect signs of infection to reduce the possible risks and treat the disease more efficiently. This method is most significant in preventing which of the following?

A) West Nile Virus: A virus spread by mosquitoes which is the leading cause of mosquito-borne disease in the continental United States

B) Meningitis: An inflammation of the protective membranes covering the brain and spinal cord.

C) Hepatitis B: A serious infection of the liver which increases the risk of developing liver failure, liver cancer or cirrhosis

D) Encephalitis: An inflammation of the brain tissue.

66

An inflammatory response is usually activated after an injury. Which of the following symptoms is not a sign of inflammation?

A) Pain

B) Redness

C) Bleeding

D) Lose of function

CONTINUE ▶

67

Decomposing organic matter recycles various organic materials otherwise regarded as waste products.

Which of the following processes decomposes plant remains into humus by naturally occurring soil bacteria?

A) Mulching
B) Reducing
C) Conserving
D) Composting

68

Patients exhibiting symptoms of flu have been increasing and are being treated by the health-care practitioners in the community. However, the patients do not respond to any of the standard medications for the treatment of flu.

In this case, which of the following agencies should these practitioners contact for assistance?

A) American Medical Association
B) Center for Drug Evaluation and Research
C) American Pharmacists Association
D) Centers for Disease Control and Prevention

69

There are ten main systems in the human body, and each has different roles.

Which of the following system serves as the first line of defense of the body against infection?

A) Integumentary system
B) Respiratory system
C) Lymphatic system
D) Immune system

70

A **doctor** is a person skilled in the field of medicine and trained and licensed to cure sick and injured people.

Which of the following types of doctor primarily serves the elderly community?

A) Obstetrician
B) Pediatrician
C) Geriatrician
D) Toxicologist

CONTINUE ▶

71

The Center for Disease Control Prevention (CDC) developed a framework known as the Whole School, Whole Community, Whole Child (WSCC) model, to address health in schools. WSCC has ten (10) components.

Which of the following components considers the school's physical and aesthetic surroundings?

A) Nutrition services
B) Physical environment
C) Emotional climate
D) Psychological and social services

72

Prozac is an antidepressant which is also known as fluoxetine. It is mainly used to treat major depression, panic disorder, and obsessive-compulsive disorder.

Which of the following neurotransmitters (chemical substance which is released at the end of a nerve after the arrival of an impulse) is most affected by the antidepressant Prozac?

A) Adrenaline
B) Serotonin
C) Cortisol
D) Epinephrine

73

Fetal alcohol syndrome is a condition in children that results from alcohol consumption or exposure during a woman's pregnancy. This disorder is related to which of the following?

A) Developmental disabilities: A group of conditions due to an impairment in physical, learning, language, or behavior areas.
B) Hepatitis: An inflammation of the liver which is highly contagious.
C) Anemia: A condition in which the blood doesn't have enough healthy red blood cells.
D) Leukemia: A cancer of blood-forming tissues, hindering the ability of the body to fight infection.

CONTINUE ▶

74

Waste treatment refers to the activities required to ensure that waste has the least possible impact on the environment.

Which of the following best describes the primary objective of Reduce, Reuse, and Recycle in waste treatment hierarchy?

A) Giving incentives in regards to the correct allocation of non-hazardous wastes, both commercial and industrial.

B) Combine the spillover costs of a particular product into its market price.

C) Gain a maximum benefit from products and at the same time, making a minimal amount of waste.

D) Guarantee that costs of waste disposal are paid fairly by the waste generators.

75

In an emergency, which of the following options is the most practical way to guarantee that an accident victim gets a medical response immediately?

A) Communicating with a medical expert with relevant medication skills.

B) Calling the nearest hospital.

C) Calling 911 on the phone.

D) Contacting the office of the victim's chief care physician.

76

Which of the following is the leading cause of death for both men and women in the U.S. and in the world?

A) Cardiovascular disease

B) Cancer

C) HIV or AIDS

D) Accidents and violence-related events

CONTINUE ▶

77

Which of the following best states why alcohol use increases the chance of injury for people involved in recreational activities?

A) Alcohol use heightens sensory perception and causes substantial exaggerated responses.

B) Alcoholic beverages contain elements that hasten metabolism.

C) Alcoholic drinks contain ethanol or ethyl alcohol, a type of psychoactive drug.

D) Alcohol usage weakens motor reflexes and slows down time reception.

78

Lea, an 18-year old girl, is experiencing compulsive eating in large amounts.

Which of the following conditions does Lea most likely have?

A) Bulimia nervosa

B) Binge eating disorder

C) Orthorexia Nervosa

D) Anorexia nervosa

79

Ephedra is an herb that may stimulate the heart, lungs or the nervouse system due to the ephedrine it contains. It is usually added to some herbal supplements, however, an increased risk for a particular health problem has been shown associated with the use of Ephedra.

Which of the following health problem is being referred in the statement given above?

A) Brain damage

B) Cardiac arrest

C) Congenital disabilities

D) Stomach cancer

80

Tay-Sachs disease is a genetic disorder that destroys the nerve cells in the brain and spinal cord. This disease is most prevalent in which of the following populations?

A) North Americans

B) South Americans

C) Asians

D) European Jews

CONTINUE ▶

81

Which of the following is representing an incorrect statement?

A) Water comprises 70% or more of the bodies of animals.

B) Fats yield the most significant amount of energy.

C) Proteins are the facilitators of growth and repair of animal cells and are also a form of reserved energy.

D) Carbohydrates are the least essential type of nutrient the body needs.

82

Minerals needed by the body can be classified as macrominerals (those needed in large amounts) and trace minerals (those needed in small amounts).

Which of the following statements is correct about minerals?

A) Both zinc and sodium are trace minerals.

B) Both zinc and sodium are macrominerals

C) Zinc is a trace mineral while sodium is a macromineral.

D) Zinc is a macromineral while sodium is a trace mineral.

83

Sulfur dioxide and nitrogen oxide emission causes acid rain by reacting with the water molecules in the atmosphere to produce acids.

Which of the following about the acid rains is not correct?

A) Ammonia is produced by the reaction of sulfurous gases such as sulfur dioxide with water.
B) Deceased fish and wildlife populations, damaged bodies of water, as well as human health hazards has been linked by scientific evidence to acid rain.
C) Acid rain is a 1980s household term used when emissions from the industry and motor vehicles were being blamed for causing environmental deterioration.
D) Acid rain results from air pollution since sulfur dioxide and nitrogen oxides are bi-products of burning fuels in electric utilities as well as other industrial and natural sources.

84

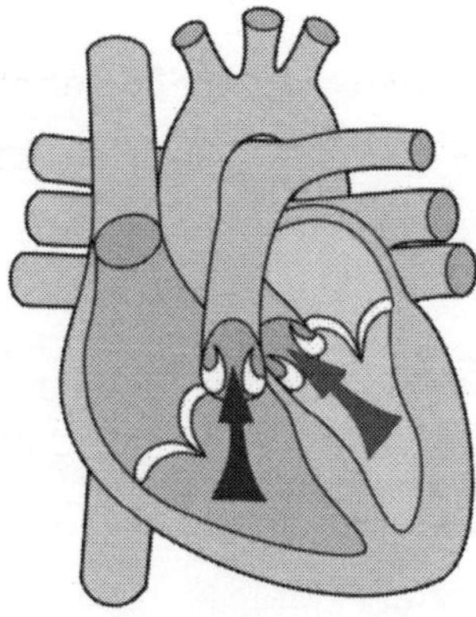

The term used to describe the amount of blood the heart pumps through the circulatory system within a minute is **cardiac output**. On the other hand, stroke volume is the amount of blood put out by the left ventricle of the heart in one contraction. In general, the stroke volume and the heart rate regulate the cardiac output.

How can cardiac output (Q) be measured?

A) The quantity of oxygen consumed times the heart's rate of pumping.
B) The quantity of oxygen consumed times the pressure exerted against the arterial walls.
C) The quantity of blood ejected with each beat times the pressure exerted against the artery walls.
D) The quantity of blood ejected with each beat times the heart's rate of pumping.

CONTINUE ▶

85

Anabolism, constructive metabolism, is the synthesis of complex molecules in living organisms from simpler ones together with the storage of energy.

Which of the following is an example of anabolism?

A) The disintegration of proteins into amino acids
B) Disintegration of large molecules into smaller molecules
C) Forming of small molecules from large molecules
D) Forming of proteins from amino acids

86

The 33 individual, interlocking bones that form the spinal column is called the **vertebrae.**

Which of the following is not correct about vertebrae?

A) There are twelve thoracic vertebrae from the middle to upper back.
B) Five lunar vertebrae make up the lower back.
C) There are seven cervical vertebrae in the neck region.
D) There are five sacral vertebrae, which are fused together.

87

Carbohydrates serve as the immediate energy source of our body. Corns, wheat, oats, and barley fall in which of the following classification of carbohydrates?

A) Glycogen
B) Starch
C) Glycoprotein
D) Oligosaccharide

88

A **personality disorder** refers to a long-term pattern of thinking and behavior that causes distress, making it difficult to function in everyday life.

In other words, which of the following best describes the condition?

A) Personality disorders are maladaptive ways of perceiving, thinking, and relating.
B) Personality disorders are the person's reactions to stress.
C) Personality disorders are episodic in nature.
D) Personality disorders are intra-psychic disturbances.

CONTINUE ▶

89

In human beings, the homeostatic regulation of body temperature involves such mechanisms as sweating when the internal temperature becomes excessive and shivering to produce heat, as well as the generation of heat through metabolic processes when the internal temperature falls too low.

Which of the following is not included in homeostatic mechanisms in the body?

A) Respiration
B) Osmoregulation
C) Excretion
D) Thermoregulation

90

Vitamins are essential micronutrients that are needed by an organism.

Which of the following statements is correct regarding vitamins?

A) Vitamin A is a water-soluble vitamin while Vitamin C is a fat-soluble vitamin.
B) Vitamin A is a fat-soluble vitamin while Vitamin C is a water-soluble vitamin.
C) Both Vitamin A and Vitamin B are fat-soluble vitamins.
D) Both Vitamin A and Vitamin B are water-soluble vitamins

CONTINUE ▶

91

Alcoholism is the term used for any drinking of alcohol that results in mental or physical health problems.

Which of the following describes alcoholism?

A) Hard-drinking on weekends
B) Alcohol intolerance
C) The inability to control the amount a person drinks.
D) None of the above

92

Alcoholic beverages are drinks that contain a considerable amount of ethanol which is considered as a depressant.

As alcohol enters the body, in which of the following body organs is it metabolized?

A) In the liver
B) In the stomach
C) In the kidneys
D) In the brain

93

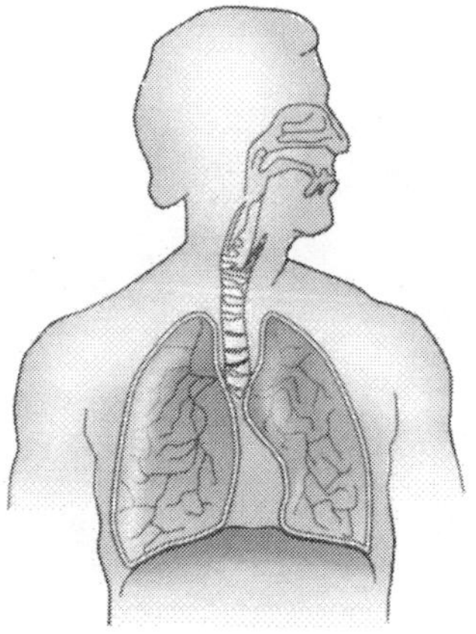

A person's number of breaths per minute is called **respiratory rate**. If a person has 25 breaths per minute, it is considered as abnormal.

Which of the following respiratory rate is considered to be normal?

A) 16 to 20 breaths per minute
B) 22 to 26 breaths per minute
C) 30 to 36 breaths per minute
D) 6 to 10 breaths per minute

94

The main purpose of aerobic endurance training is to enhance and preserve the fitness of the cardiovacscular system of the body. Aerobic endurance training has different types.

Which of the following is not one of the aerobic endurance training exercises.

A) Sequencing
B) Pace
C) Repetition
D) Slow distance training

95

Human activities are partly responsible for changes in global temperatures experienced during the past 100 years.

Which of the following best explains why average global temperatures over the last 100 years is so high?

A) Natural systems do not generally shift that quickly unless disturbed by some external mechanism.
B) Natural systems are always changing, but generally at an almost constant rate.
C) Natural systems usually show randomly fluctuating rates of change over time.
D) Natural systems usually show decreasing rates of change as the system matures.

96

Which of the following is not defined correctly?

A) The epidermis is the thin, top layer of the skin that contains blood vessels, lymph vessels, hair follicles, and glands.
B) Sebum is an oily substance that is secreted by the sebaceous glands that help keep the skin and hair moisturized.
C) Collagen is is the most abundant protein in our bodies which gives our skin strength and elasticity.
D) Keratin is found in hair, horns, claws, hooves, and the outer layer of human skin which serves as a waterproofing protein in the skin.

CONTINUE ▶

SECTION 3 - GENERAL HEALTH

#	Answer	Topic	Subtopic
1	B	TC	SC6
2	C	TB	SB4
3	C	TC	SC7
4	A	TC	SC2
5	B	TB	SB4
6	A	TC	SC4
7	A	TC	SC3
8	A	TC	SC3
9	A	TC	SC4
10	B	TC	SC6
11	C	TC	SC7
12	B	TB	SB4
13	A	TC	SC6
14	B	TC	SC6
15	D	TC	SC1
16	A	TC	SC3
17	D	TC	SC4
18	B	TC	SC7
19	C	TC	SC6
20	C	TC	SC5
21	A	TB	SB4
22	B	TC	SC7
23	C	TC	SC3
24	D	TC	SC6

#	Answer	Topic	Subtopic
25	B	TC	SC5
26	C	TB	SB4
27	A	TC	SC4
28	C	TC	SC2
29	B	TC	SC4
30	B	TB	SB4
31	D	TC	SC4
32	A	TC	SC4
33	B	TC	SC3
34	C	TB	SB4
35	C	TB	SB4
36	C	TC	SC2
37	C	TC	SC1
38	C	TC	SC7
39	D	TC	SC7
40	D	TC	SC7
41	A	TC	SC7
42	B	TC	SC2
43	B	TB	SB4
44	B	TC	SC7
45	A	TC	SC7
46	A	TC	SC2
47	D	TC	SC5
48	D	TC	SC7

#	Answer	Topic	Subtopic
49	B	TC	SC3
50	A	TC	SC4
51	B	TB	SB4
52	D	TB	SB4
53	B	TC	SC2
54	B	TC	SC7
55	B	TC	SC3
56	B	TC	SC2
57	B	TB	SB4
58	D	TC	SC4
59	D	TC	SC5
60	D	TB	SB4
61	D	TC	SC1
62	B	TC	SC6
63	B	TC	SC3
64	B	TB	SB4
65	C	TC	SC7
66	C	TC	SC7
67	D	TC	SC5
68	D	TC	SC3
69	A	TC	SC6
70	C	TC	SC7
71	B	TC	SC3
72	B	TC	SC2

#	Answer	Topic	Subtopic
73	A	TC	SC2
74	C	TC	SC5
75	C	TC	SC7
76	A	TC	SC1
77	D	TC	SC2
78	B	TC	SC4
79	B	TC	SC4
80	D	TC	SC7
81	D	TC	SC4
82	C	TC	SC4
83	A	TC	SC5
84	D	TC	SC6
85	C	TC	SC4
86	B	TC	SC6
87	B	TC	SC4
88	A	TC	SC2
89	A	TC	SC6
90	B	TC	SC4
91	C	TC	SC1
92	A	TC	SC6
93	A	TC	SC6
94	A	TB	SB4
95	A	TC	SC5
96	A	TC	SC6

Topics & Subtopics

Code	Description
SB4	Health-Related Physical Fitness
SC1	Personal Health
SC2	Mental & Emotional Health
SC3	Community Health
SC4	Nutrition Health

Code	Description
SC5	Environmental Health
SC6	Anatomy & Physiology
SC7	Health Promotion & Prevention of Injury and Diseases
TB	Physical Education
TC	General Health

CONTINUE ▶

Made in the USA
Middletown, DE
15 July 2020

12736428R00064